Mike Meyers' Guide to Supporting Windows® 7 for CompTIA A+® Certification

(Exams 220-701 & 220-702)

Mike Meyers' Guide to Supporting Windows® 7 for CompTIA A+® Certification

(Exams 220-701 & 220-702)

Mike Meyers

New York • Chicago • San Francisco • Lisbon
London • Madrid • Mexico City • Milan • New Delhi
San Juan • Seoul • Singapore • Sydney • Toronto

The McGraw·Hill Companies

Cataloging-in-Publication Data is on file with the Library of Congress

McGraw-Hill books are available at special quantity discounts to use as premiums and sales promotions, or for use in corporate training programs. To contact a representative, please e-mail us at bulksales@mcgraw-hill.com.

Mike Meyers' Guide to Supporting Windows® 7 for CompTIA A+® Certification
(Exams 220-701 & 220-702)

1234567890   QFR QFR   10987654321

ISBN: Book p/n 978-0-07-176389-9 and CD p/n 978-0-07-176390-5
of set 978-0-07-176392-9

MHID: Book p/n 0-07-176389-9 and CD p/n 0-07-176390-2
of set 0-07-176392-9

Sponsoring Editor	**Technical Editor**	**Composition**
Timothy Green	*Christopher A. Crayton*	*Cenveo Publisher Services*
Editorial Supervisor	**Copy Editor**	**Illustration**
Jody McKenzie	*LeeAnn Pickrell*	*Cenveo Publisher Services*
Project Editor	**Proofreader**	**Art Director, Cover**
Emilia Thiuri, Fortuitous Publishing Services	*Emilia Thiuri*	*Jeff Weeks*
	Indexer	
Acquisitions Coordinator	*Jack Lewis*	
Stephanie Evans		
	Production Supervisor	
	James Kussow	

I dedicate this book to all the up and coming techs out there.

ABOUT THE AUTHOR

Mike Meyers, lovingly called the "AlphaGeek" by those who know him, is the industry's leading authority on CompTIA A+ certification. He is the president and cofounder of Total Seminars, LLC, a provider of PC and network repair seminars, books, videos, and courseware for thousands of organizations throughout the world. Mike has been involved in the computer and network repair industry since 1977 as a technician, instructor, author, consultant, and speaker. Author of numerous popular books and videos, including the best-selling *CompTIA A+ Certification All-in-One Exam Guide*, Mike is also the series editor for the highly successful Mike Meyers' Certification Passport series, the Mike Meyers' Computer Skills series, and the Mike Meyers' Guide To series, all published by McGraw-Hill. As well as writing, Mike has personally taught (and continues to teach) thousands of students, including U.S. senators and U.S. Supreme Court justices; members of the United Nations, every branch of the U.S. Armed Forces, and most branches of the Department of Justice; plus hundreds of corporate clients, academic students at every level, prisoners, and pensioners.

E-mail: michaelm@totalsem.com
Facebook: Mike Meyers (Houston, TX)
Twitter/Skype/most instant messaging clients: desweds
Web forums: www.totalsem.com/forums

About the Technical Editor

Christopher A. Crayton (MCSE, MCP+I, CompTIA A+, CompTIA Network+) is an author, technical editor, technical consultant, security consultant, and trainer. Formerly a computer and networking instructor at Keiser College (2001 Teacher of the Year), Chris has also worked as network administrator for Protocol and at Eastman Kodak Headquarters as a computer and network specialist. Chris has authored several print and online books on topics ranging from CompTIA A+ and CompTIA Security+ to Microsoft Windows Vista. Chris has provided technical edits and reviews for many publishers, including McGraw-Hill, Pearson Education, Charles River Media, Cengage Learning, Wiley, O'Reilly, Syngress, and Apress.

CONTENTS AT A GLANCE

CONTENTS

ACKNOWLEDGMENTS

Aaron Verber, my in-house editor, made his mark on this book from beginning to end. His dedication and creativity helped hammer wrought iron text into a shimmering sword of prose. Thank you.

Tim Green, my acquisitions editor, guided me with a surprisingly calm voice toward finishing this book. His motivation was greatly appreciated.

Chris Crayton continues to astound and amaze with his technical editing wizardry. His attention to detail helped straighten out every last glitch in this book.

Scott Jernigan, my Editor-in-Chief, helped keep this project on track with charm and grace, even as his own computer self-destructed before our eyes. Thank you, as always, for your linguistic guile.

Ford Pierson's line art illustrations are top-notch, as usual. I continue to be amazed by his hard work and artistic flexibility. His skill and patience are unmatched. Thank you!

Michael Smyer's photographs are, once again, outstanding. His encyclopedic grasp of technology makes writing this book both a challenge and a joy, much to the benefit of the final product. Great job, Michael.

At McGraw-Hill Professional, the team once again proved their excellence. With a polite attitude and several gentle nudges toward my deadlines, they were a big help.

Stephanie Evans, the acquisitions coordinator, kept me up to date and on track. Her coordination skills are second to none. It was great working with you.

Jody McKenzie was the editorial supervisor. It was nice working with you again.

Emilia Thiuri did a great job coordinating the editing phase of the project. Her efficiency and keen eye helped carry this book to the finish line.

To the copy editor LeeAnn Pickrell and the compositor, Cenveo—thank you for everything you contributed to this book. Excellent work.

Why Did CompTIA Make This Update?

In August of 2010, CompTIA shocked the IT training industry by announcing their intent to add Windows 7 to the already existing 220-701 and 220-702 exams. This was big news. Never before had CompTIA changed the objectives of an existing exam. CompTIA's motivation for this unprecedented move was simple: to keep their ISO recognition in order to sell the CompTIA exams. This move also enabled the CompTIA A+ exams to actually cover the latest version of Windows. Windows 7 came out right after the previous CompTIA A+ update (back in 2009), instantly putting the exams behind the curve.

 NOTE The 2009 update wasn't the first time CompTIA got caught missing the latest version of Windows. When CompTIA updated the exams in 2006, they just missed the introduction of Vista. Thank goodness this update happened—we're up to date for the first time in five years!

When Did This Update Take Effect?

This update took effect January 1st, 2011. New questions were added to the existing 220-701 and 220-702 exams, so there are no old exams to retire. The 2009 bridge exam (BR0-003) was not updated. It was retired on December 31st, 2010.

This Is Not Just a Windows 7 Update!

While CompTIA is making a lot of noise announcing the inclusion of Windows 7, a careful check of the objectives show there's more to this update than just Windows 7! Some of the "not just Windows 7" areas are:

- Basic understanding of IPv6 addressing
- Basic understanding of the FAT64 (exFAT) file system
- User Account Control (Already in Vista but improved in Windows 7)
- Network discovery (Already in Vista but improved in Windows 7)

What Do We Need to Know about Windows 7?

The most important item to understand is that there will be a number of questions using the term "Windows 7" that won't have anything to do with Windows 7. Consider a question like this:

Timmy installs a second SATA drive into his Windows 7 system. When he reboots, which application should he use to create new volumes on the drive?

    A. FDISK

    B. Disk Management

    C. CMOS Setup

    D. CHKDSK

The correct answer is Disk Management. However, this would be the correct answer even if Timmy used Windows XP or Windows Vista.

 TECH TIP   If you understand Windows XP and Vista, you understand *most* of what you need to know for Windows 7. This book covers only unique Windows 7 topics!

I've broken down the unique CompTIA A+ Windows 7 topics into seven major areas:

1. Understanding the differences between the Windows 7 interface and the Windows Vista interface. This includes changes to Windows Explorer, the inclusion of libraries, and the introduction of exFAT (FAT64).

2. Learning how to prepare for a Windows 7 installation. This includes preinstallation tasks, such as using the Windows Upgrade Advisor, and preparing your hard drive for state-of-the-art file systems.

3. Understanding how Windows 7 boots, issues that may be encountered during a boot up, and tools used to correct boot problems.

4. Understanding how Windows 7's User Account Control (UAC) differs from UAC in Windows Vista.

5. Learning about the new IPv6 networking protocol and how it compares to IPv4.

6. Understanding networking in Windows 7, including the new HomeGroup feature and how it applies to features already in Windows Vista.

7. Troubleshooting Windows 7 using new and improved tools found in Control Panel.

How This Book Is Organized

This book is designed for two different types of students. The first is someone who prepared (using any study guide) for the "old" CompTIA A+ 220-701 and 220-702 exams. The second is someone who is still using *CompTIA A+ Certification All-in-One Exam Guide, 7th Edition, Mike Meyers' CompTIA A+ Guide to Managing and Troubleshooting PCs, 3rd Edition*, or the exam-specific books, including *Mike Meyers' CompTIA A+ Guide: Essentials, 3rd Edition* and *Mike Meyers' CompTIA A+ Guide: Practical Application, 3rd Edition*.

The beginning of each chapter in this book contains a list that references one or more of the books mentioned above. Each listing includes an abbreviation and a chapter number. The abbreviations tell you which book to check and the chapter numbers indicate the chapter in that book. Sound confusing? Not really. Table 1 will help you sort it all out. I've added pictures of the book covers to make sure you know which book you're using.

Here's an example:

This chapter ties into what you learned from
All-in-One: Chapter 4
Managing and Troubleshooting: Chapter 6
Meyers' Guide to 702: Chapter 2

What's the Deal With "No More Lifetime Certification?"

In early 2010, CompTIA announced that, effective January 1st, 2011, CompTIA A+, CompTIA Network+, and CompTIA Security+ certifications are no longer considered "Certified for Life." If you passed any of these exams before the deadline, you're still certified for life. Going forward, you'll need to either retake the exam every three years or perform some type of continuing education.

Retaking the exams isn't that hard to understand, but the continuing education is a bit more complex. We'll review it in the following section, which the CompTIA website includes a helpful table from (http://www.comptia.org/certifications/listed/renewal.aspx).

Continuing Education Requirements

How many continuing education units are required to renew my certification? For a candidate to renew CompTIA A+ requires 20 CEUs; to renew CompTIA Network+, 30 CEUs; and to renew CompTIA Security+, 50 CEUs.

Book Title	Cover	Abbreviation
CompTIA A+ Certification All-in-One Exam Guide, 7th Edition		All-in-One
Mike Meyers' CompTIA A+ Guide to Managing and Troubleshooting PCs, 3rd Edition		Managing and Troubleshooting
Mike Meyers' CompTIA A+ Guide: Essentials, 3rd Edition		Meyers' Guide to 701
Mike Meyers' CompTIA A+ Guide: Practical Application, 3rd Edition		Meyers' Guide to 702

Table 1 A+ Book Abbreviations

The following chart details the requirements for continuing units:

Activity	Credits	Required Submission
Teaching, lecturing or presenting industry content relevant to the highest level CompTIA certification achieved	Each hour of material creation: 2 CEUs Each hour of delivery: 1 CEU	Proof of session participation, completion of session detail form (topic, date, time venue, attendee details)
Participating in non-degree courses or computer-based training using CAQC-approved materials	1 CEU per hour of validated training	Proof of completion of class or Web-based session, including proof of vendor, training description, number of hours completed and assessment score achieved
Attendance at relevant industry event, seminar or conference	1 CEU per hour spent in relevant sessions	Proof of attendance, with brief submission of sessions attended and summary of primary information gained (100 word minimum per session)
Participation in relevant CompTIA exam development workshop	10 CEUs per workshop completion	Form submitted from development session coordinator confirming full completion
Publishing a relevant industry article, white paper, blog or book	Article or white paper: 4 CEUs Blog: 1 CEU Book: 20 CEUs	Reference to published work; work must be credited to candidate. Articles and white papers, minimum 4 pages; blog on technical site, minimum 1,000 words; book, minimum 150 pages
Obtaining an industry certification relevant to the highest level CompTIA certification achieved	15/20/40 CEUs for CompTIA A+, CompTIA Network+ or CompTIA Security+, respectively	Proof of certification from certification body
Completing industry-related college courses from degree-granting institution	10 CEUs per completion of 3-4 credit hours	Transcript, including class taken, timeframe grade and number of credits

*Activities and continuing education requirements are subject to change.

Note the asterisk at the end of the table—I have strong suspicion these requirements will change once CompTIA realizes the amount of work they're creating for themselves. Seriously, who is going to read your 1000-word report on "What I Learned at XYZ Conference?" Now that you have the Web link, be sure to check for yourself.

 NOTE There's lots of detailed information about the new three-year certification on the Web site listed earlier. Take some time to read it.

Personally, I think this is a long overdue feature. Someone who took the Comp-TIA A+ exam in 2010 had no way to distinguish themselves from a person who took the exam in 1997, and that wasn't fair. CompTIA's certifications are now in line with Microsoft, Cisco, and other industry certifications.

Enjoy the reading! I'm a huge fan of Windows 7. If you're not entirely sold on Windows 7 yet, this book might just change your mind. As always, if you need to contact me, my e-mail address is desweds@gmail.com. I'm also on both Facebook and Twitter under my codename "desweds."

Mike Meyers

CHAPTER 1

Meet Windows 7

This chapter ties into what you learned from

- **All-In-One:** Chapter 4
- **Managing and Troubleshooting:** Chapter 4
- **Meyers' Guide to 701:** Chapter 4

Comparing the look and feel of Windows Vista to Windows 7 might make you think that the two operating systems are far more alike than different. Microsoft made a lot of changes to Vista's interface, making it much shinier and sleeker than its predecessor, Windows XP. The taskbar, Start button, menus, and many common utilities all received a new coat of paint. Windows 7 continues the same look and feel introduced by Windows Vista but reduces many of its complexities.

If Windows Vista and Windows 7 look and act so much alike, why didn't Microsoft just call Windows 7 "Windows Vista: The Fixed Version?" Well, like any "1.0" product, Vista received (at least in this humble author's opinion) very negative reactions when Microsoft rolled it out back in 2007. Granted, Vista went through some teething problems, but the basic idea was solid. By the time Microsoft revealed the "fixed" version, nobody wanted anything to do with Vista. Microsoft didn't have a choice; they had to call this "fixed" Vista something new. Enter Windows 7.

In this chapter, I'll introduce you to the differences between the Windows Vista and the Windows 7 interfaces. We'll start with changes to the taskbar and notification area, and then look at libraries in Windows Explorer. We'll then turn to the transition from the Sidebar to desktop gadgets. The chapter finishes with a look at a new file system, called exFAT.

As you learn about the changes, take a moment to notice this very important fact: Windows Vista and Windows 7 are very similar. The CompTIA A+ exams include questions that might say "Windows Vista" or "Windows 7," but you need to know that the answers will likely be the same regardless.

Comparing Desktops—The Taskbar

Windows 7 unveiled some subtle but important changes to the Windows Desktop, both superficial and technological. Let's start with the taskbar. Although the taskbar in Windows Vista introduced the rounded start button and a new default look, it worked almost identically to the old Windows XP taskbar. In particular, Vista retained the Quick Launch toolbar and notification area from Windows XP (although they looked nicer), as seen in Figure 1-1.

Figure 1-1
Windows Vista
taskbar

Windows 7 dumped the Quick Launch toolbar and replaced it with the pinned-icon concept. A *pinned icon* represents an open or closed program that attaches to the taskbar. To pin a program, start it. You'll see the program on the taskbar. Right-click the program on the taskbar to see the menu (Microsoft calls this the *Jump List*), as shown in Figure 1-2, and select *Pin this program to taskbar*. Now even if you close the program completely, the icon stays on the taskbar.

Figure 1-2   Pinning a program to the taskbar using the Jump List

 NOTE   You can also pin executables and shortcuts by right-clicking them and selecting Pin to Taskbar.

Look closely at Figure 1-3: Notice that some of the programs show themselves inside a highlighted rectangle whereas others don't. Windows highlights running programs.

Figure 1-3   Windows 7 taskbar showing pinned and unpinned icons

 TECH TIP   Unpinning an icon is trivial. Just right-click it to bring up the Jump List and select *Unpin this program from taskbar*.

The Windows XP and Windows Vista taskbars suffered from messiness because each running program took up more and more space. An option available in the taskbar preferences combined multiple copies of a single program (like multiple Microsoft

Word documents, for example) into a single area on the taskbar, as shown in Figure 1-4, but not everyone took advantage of this option.

 TECH TIP   The official Microsoft term for each copy of an open application is an *instance*.

If your graphics card supported DirectX version 9, Vista added a preview of the open program (as Figure 1-4 also shows), but if more than one instance was open, it only showed the top one.

Figure 1-4
Windows Vista
preview Window

Windows 7 improved on Vista's preview idea by adding a new feature called *Aero Peek*. Aero Peek does two very cool things. First, if you place the cursor over a program in the taskbar, it shows you a preview of each running instance, not just the top one (see Figure 1-5). Second, if you move the mouse cursor to one of the preview windows, the full window appears on the desktop and all other windows fade into the background (Figure 1-6). Be sure to notice exactly where the mouse pointers are located in each of these figures.

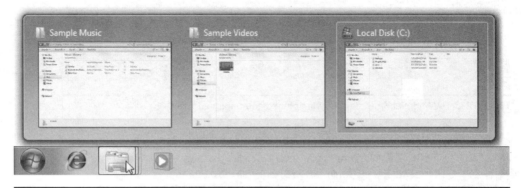

Figure 1-5   Aero Peek showing multiple instances of a program

If you thought the word "Aero" in Aero Peek implies you need to use the Aero desktop to take advantage of this feature, you are correct. Unlike Vista's version of Aero, however, Windows 7 treats the Aero desktop as the default mode. To enjoy the power

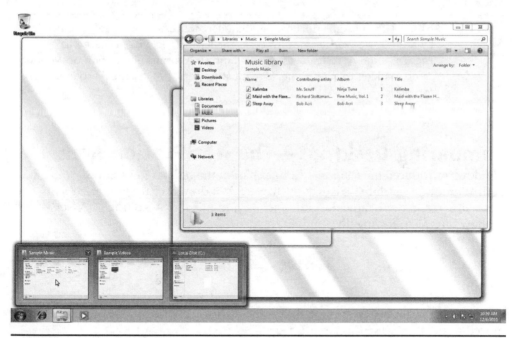

Figure 1-6   Aero Peek showing a program preview

of Windows 7 fully, you need a video card that can handle the requirements of Aero desktop. Windows 7 installs DirectX 11 on your system, but your video card only needs to support DirectX 9 to use Aero.

Windows 7 Aero desktop doesn't stop at Aero Peek. Aero desktop also includes two other features: Aero Shake and Aero Snap. Table 1-1 describes these two features, as well as Aero Peek.

Feature	Description
Aero Peek	You can highlight an application in the taskbar to reveal a preview window of that application.
Aero Shake	You can shake any window to minimize all the other windows; shake the same window again and all the other windows return to their original locations.
Aero Snap	You can move a window to the left or right edge of your screen to make it snap to fill exactly that half of your screen. Resize the bottom (or top) of a window to the bottom (or top) of the monitor and your windows will take up the entire height of the screen (but keep the same width).

Table 1-1   New Aero Features in Windows 7

You need to use an Aero theme to enable most of Aero's features. To switch themes, go to Start | Control Panel | Appearance and Personalization | Personalization.

EXAM TIP In some documentation, Microsoft calls the three Aero features by their single word names, so *Peek*, *Shake*, and *Snap*. Be prepared to recognize the Aero features on the CompTIA exams either with or without "Aero" added to their name. Like most writers, I've left the Aero in this text for clarity.

Comparing Desktops—The Notification Area

Windows introduced the *notification area* as part of the taskbar in Windows 95, and, up until Windows 7, it didn't change much. Sure, Windows XP hid little-used icons, but that's all it could do to tame the glut of icons, and this remained true for Vista as well, as shown in the following illustration.

If you right-click a Vista machine's taskbar and select Properties, you'll see a tab called Notification Area. You could find these settings in Windows XP, too; Vista simply moved some of those settings to this new tab.

If you're like me and have a lot of background programs running, those programs eat up a big part of the taskbar, especially in Windows XP, as shown in this illustration.

Vista eliminated a lot of this mess by giving you the opportunity to hide or unhide programs selectively in the notification area.

Windows 7 goes one step further by separating the notification area options from the rest of the taskbar options. Just click the tiny up arrow on the notification area and select Customize. (There's still a button you can click that will take you to these options in the regular taskbar properties if you're old school like me.)

Windows Explorer—Almost Perfect?

You can't do much on a PC without using Windows Explorer. You use Windows Explorer to poke around a computer's mass storage devices and shared resources on a network. But how often do you click the Windows Explorer icon in the Start menu? If you're like me, the answer is not that often. Instead, you probably use the My Documents folder, the Computer icon—even the Recycle Bin—but Windows Explorer actually powers all of these things, too.

Before Vista, Windows Explorer wasn't very sophisticated. It performed well enough, but Vista brought some big changes to the power and interface of Windows Explorer. Windows 7 takes Windows Explorer to a new level, incorporating features like the powerful new libraries. In this section, we'll compare and contrast Windows Explorer in Vista and Windows 7 and take a close look at the new libraries feature in Windows 7.

Touring Windows Explorer

Every time you open a folder or click Computer, you open Windows Explorer. You can, however, run Windows Explorer in its "pure" form by typing **Windows Explorer** into the Vista/7 Start search box (or by opening Windows Explorer in the Start menu under Accessories or by right-clicking the Start button and clicking Open Windows Explorer). To start our comparison, let's open Windows Explorer in both Vista and 7. In Vista, you'll see something like this:

Firing up Computer on a typical Windows 7 machine shows something like this:

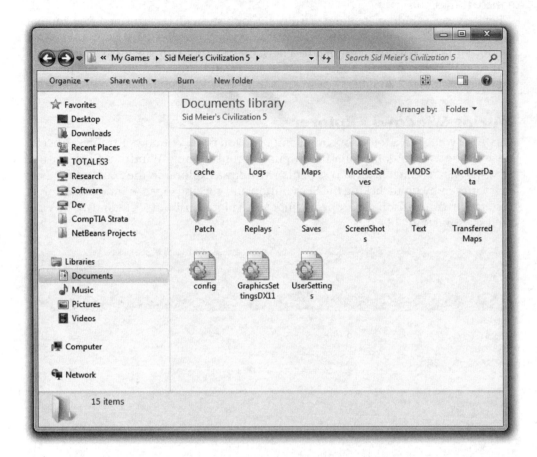

Windows Vista replaced XP's address bar with a "bread crumb" address bar and switched the badly dated menu bar with a ribbon-style toolbar. The bread crumb address bar enables you to march up a directory structure by clicking where you want to go. For example, if the address bar points to C:\Users\mike\Downloads and you want to go to C:\Users\mike, just click "mike" and you're there! Bread crumb address bars were a great feature in Vista's Windows Explorer and Windows 7 retains that handy feature.

The new address bar worked great, but Microsoft faced a challenge with the menu bar. Microsoft wanted Windows Explorer to work for just about anything from using the Recycle Bin to burning a DVD, but these two items are very different. Microsoft needed a Windows Explorer toolbar that changed for different types of storage. To that end, they created the ribbon-style toolbar. The toolbar gave Microsoft a place for

Figure 1-7 Two different Windows Explorers in Vista

device-specific options. Figure 1-7 shows two open folders in Vista's Windows Explorer. Note how the toolbar changes to reflect the needs of each storage option. In fact, the toolbar even changes based on the type of data selected!

EXAM TIP Make sure you know how to show hidden files in each version of Windows Explorer. In 2000/XP, you can find the option in Tools | Folder Options. Windows Vista and Windows 7, however, tuck it under Organize | Folder and search options.

Windows 7 made a number of minor changes to the location of various options in the toolbar. In Windows 7, for example, Microsoft moved the slider to change the default icon size from the Views option on the left of the toolbar to a simple icon on the right. Despite these small changes, the function of the Windows Explorer toolbars between Windows Vista and Windows 7 remains the same.

Enter Libraries

Windows 7 introduced only one new—but very useful—feature to Windows Explorer: libraries. The idea behind libraries is based on two fairly straightforward assumptions:

- People tend to need the same data over and over.
- The data you need for one job/project/function/whatever is rarely stored in a single folder.

Windows Explorer has long supported the first assumption. Even back in the Dark Ages of computing (Windows 2000), you could create a shortcut to just about any single file or folder. The downside to shortcuts is that folks tend to create a lot of them, making Desktops messy. To make our lives easier and better looking, Windows XP's Windows Explorer added the concept of favorites. A *favorite* is basically a shortcut that's stored in Windows Explorer's Task Pane instead of on the desktop. The biggest benefit is that no matter how you open Windows Explorer, your favorites are always there. Figure 1-8 shows some typical favorites on a Windows Vista system.

 NOTE Favorites still exist in Windows Vista and Windows 7.

 TECH TIP Shortcut files use the extension .LNK. Favorites are pointers embedded into the registry. Shortcuts can point to individual files, whereas favorites can only point to folders.

The problem with favorites—and shortcuts—is that they only point to a single item. That's great if your life enables you to organize everything into one perfect little folder, but life isn't always that nice. In my work, for example, I take lots of photographs for my books. Sometimes I find myself wanting to reuse a photograph, and that's when libraries are handy. *Libraries* aggregate folders from multiple locations and place them in a single, easy-to-find spot in Windows Explorer. The files and folders don't actually move. The library creates links to them.

Windows 7 uses two kinds of libraries: default libraries that exist for every user and libraries you make yourself. Let's begin by learning about the very important default libraries that come with Windows 7. Once you've seen the default libraries, we'll go back to my photograph dilemma and see how libraries provide the perfect fix.

Figure 1-8   Heavily personalized favorites on a typical Vista system

Default Libraries

If you click the Start button and type in **Windows Explorer**, you'll see a screen very similar to the one shown in Figure 1-9. These are the default libraries found on every Windows 7 system.

By default, every user has four libraries: Documents, Music, Pictures, and Videos. These libraries consist of two folders: the user's My *Whatever* folder for that type of data plus the Public *Whatever* folder under c:\Users\Public. Let's clarify this subtle but critical concept with an example. Clicking the Videos library in Figure 1-9 reveals two folders, as shown in Figure 1-10.

Ignore the Sample Videos folder shown in the main pane of the Explorer window and instead concentrate on the two open folders on the left: My Videos and Public Videos. These are the two actual folders that make up this library:

C:\Users\Mike\My Videos
C:\Users\Public\Public Videos

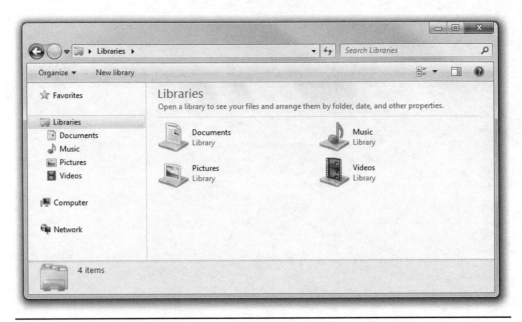

Figure 1-9   Default libraries

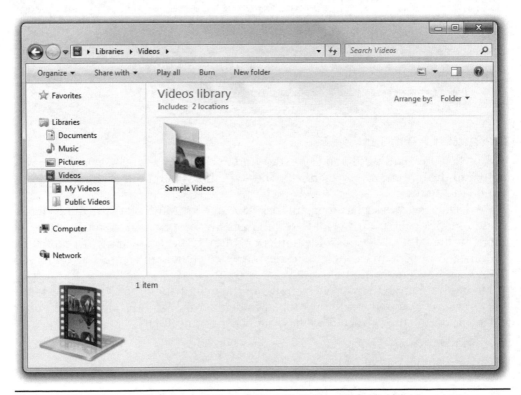

Figure 1-10   The Videos library contains two folders: My Videos and Public Videos.

The other default libraries all consist of the same two-folder setup. You might think that there's no reason to put *two* folders in by default—unless you concentrate on the word "Public." Stay tuned; libraries have a secret power that comes to life once you discover an amazing new feature of Windows 7 called homegroups—but I'm afraid you'll have to wait until Chapter 6 to learn more. Let's get back to my photograph dilemma from earlier.

Look at Figure 1-11, a photograph of a 168-pin SDRAM stick I took years ago.

Figure 1-11   A 168-pin DIMM stick

Knowing CompTIA, when it's time to update the CompTIA A+ exams again in the future, SDRAM will still be an objective, so I'll need that picture. The last time I used that image was way back in 2009, and I stored it on a file server in a folder called:

\\Server2\projects\CompTIA 220-701\Chapter 4 – RAM\Graphics\Fig04-31.TIF

Okay, great. Now when I update the book, I'll need to copy that file into a new folder called:

\\Server2\projects\CompTIA 220-801\Chapter 7 – Memory\Graphics\Fig07-21.TIF

So now I need to keep two copies. I know there are many options to choose from, but I'm very lazy, so I don't want to deal with two separate folders. With Windows 7 libraries, however, I can do something very cool. When I start my next book, I'll still create a \\Server2\projects\CompTIA 220-801\Chapter 7 – Memory\Graphics\ folder, but I'll use the library feature to link to the old \\Server2\projects\CompTIA 220-701\ Chapter 4 – RAM\Graphics\ folder. Then I can easily pick and choose photos from the older project I need without jumping back and forth between folders. So let's make a new library.

Creating Your Own Libraries

You can create a library from any instance of Windows Explorer. Right-click Libraries in the navigation pane, and then select New | Library and give it a name. Tada! You've just made your first library (Figure 1-12).

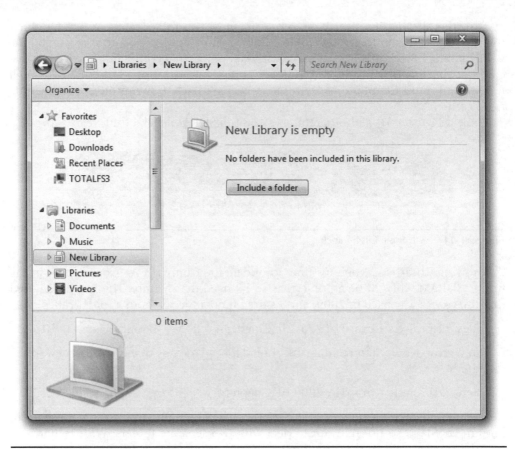

Figure 1-12   New library

Now you need to add folders to your library. You can add folders from your system or from shares on other systems. To add a folder to a library, right-click the folder, select *Include in library*, and then click the library you want to use in the fly-out menu. This only works for local folders, however. You can also right-click a library, select Properties, and use the *Include a folder* button to add folders.

Remember two important items:

- Only folders can populate a library—no individual files, no printers, etc.
- Don't try to remove a folder from a library by deleting it. If you do, you will delete the actual folder. Instead, right-click the folder name under the library name on the left and select *Remove location from library*.

Try making some libraries in Windows 7. Granted, not everyone will use them as much as I do—that's why Windows 7 still supports both favorites and shortcuts. Think of libraries as another tool to help you organize your data, no matter where it's located.

EXAM TIP   Make sure you can name the four default libraries in Windows 7.

Bye, Bye Sidebar—Hello Gadgets

Another minor but notable difference between Vista and Windows 7 is the integration of Windows Sidebar directly into the OS itself. Windows no longer includes a separate Sidebar program. If you want to add a gadget to your desktop, right-click the desktop and select Gadgets, as shown in Figure 1-13.

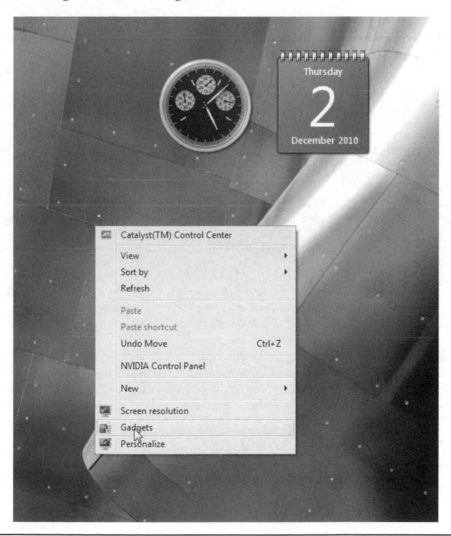

Figure 1-13   Selecting Gadgets on the desktop

Even though Sidebar is now integrated into the OS, the Windows 7 gadgets remain the same as the old Windows Vista gadgets. You still have the clock, calendar, CPU/RAM meters, and the rest of the gadgets, although the online selection is still growing.

EXAM TIP   For the CompTIA A+ exams, make sure you can add, remove, and recognize the default gadgets that come with Windows Vista and Windows 7.

Meet Your New File System

Everyone loves USB thumb drives. Their ease of use and convenience makes them indispensible for those of us who enjoy sharing a program, some photos, or a playlist. But people today want to share more than just a few small files, and they can with larger thumb drives. As thumb drives grow bigger in capacity, however, the file system becomes a problem.

The file system we have used for years on thumb drives, FAT32, does not work on drives larger than 2 terabytes (TB). Worse, FAT32 limits *file* size to 4 gigabytes (GB). Now that you can find many thumb drives larger than 2 GB, Microsoft wisely developed a replacement for FAT32.

EXAM TIP   Not only does FAT32 only support drives up to 2 TB, it only supports files up to 4 GB.

The new file system, called *exFAT* or *FAT64*, breaks the 4-GB file-size barrier, supporting drives up to 512 TB—which should be enough for a while. The exFAT file system extends FAT32 from 32-bit cluster entries to 64-bit cluster entries in the file table. Like FAT32, on the other hand, exFAT still lacks all of NTFS's extra features such as permissions, compression, and encryption.

Now, if you're like me, you might be thinking, "Why don't we just use NTFS?" And I would say, "Good point!" Microsoft, however, sees NTFS as too powerful for what most of us need from flash drives. For example, flash drives don't need NTFS permissions. But if for some reason you *really* want to format large USB thumb drives with NTFS, Windows 7 will gladly allow you to do so, as shown in Figure 1-14.

Figure 1-14
Formatting a
thumb drive in
Windows 7

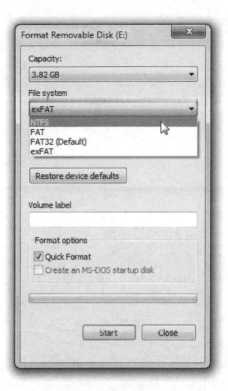

 TECH TIP   Microsoft introduced exFAT in Windows 7, but Windows Vista with SP1 also supports exFAT. Microsoft even enabled Windows XP support for exFAT with a special download (check Knowledgebase article 955704).

The Windows 7 Interface—Better Than Vista

Vista had plenty of problems when it came out. The interface, although spruced up by the visual tricks of Aero, repeated a lot of the missteps found in Windows XP. For Windows 7, however, Microsoft took those improved visuals and applied them to a number of handy new user interface elements, making the interface faster, easier to use, and Microsoft's best yet.

Chapter Review

Questions

1. Which of the following is *not* a default library?

    A. Documents

    B. Pictures

    C. Games

    D. Music

2. What is the major shortcoming of the exFAT file system?

    A. File size is limited to 4 GB.

    B. Drive size is limited to 2 TB.

    C. Does not work with Windows Vista.

    D. Lacks the many security features of NTFS.

3. What does Aero Snap do?

    A. Flips through a 3-D rendition of your open windows.

    B. Reveals open windows when you highlight an icon on the taskbar.

    C. Creates the transparent effects along the edges of windows.

    D. Resizes windows when you move or resize them in a specific way.

4. Which of the following Windows Vista taskbar features was removed from Windows 7?

    A. Start button

    B. Quick Launch toolbar

    C. Pinned icons

    D. Notification area

5. Which of the following is the biggest advantage of the ribbon-style toolbar in Windows Explorer?

    A. Device-specific options

    B. Aero transparency

    C. Libraries

    D. FAT64

6. Where do gadgets appear in Windows 7?

    A. Taskbar

    B. Notification area

    C. Sidebar

    D. Desktop

7. When you right-click a program icon on the taskbar in Windows 7, what happens?

   A. The program is added to the Pinned icons area of the Start menu.

   B. The Start menu opens.

   C. The program closes.

   D. The Jump List appears.

8. Which of the following can populate a library?

   A. Files

   B. Folders

   C. Printers

   D. All of the above

9. Which of the following is the correct path to reveal hidden files?

   A. File | Open and then select the files you want to reveal.

   B. Organize | Select all.

   C. Organize | Folder and search options | View | Show hidden files, folders, and drives.

   D. You cannot reveal hidden files. You can only reveal hidden folders and drives.

10. Which of the following versions of Windows is most like Windows 7?

    A. Windows 2000

    B. Windows XP

    C. Windows Vista

    D. Windows 98

Answers

1. **C.** By default, Windows does not include a Games library, though you could easily make one.

2. **D.** The exFAT file system improves upon FAT32 in many ways, but it still does not include the advanced security features available in NTFS.

3. **D.** Aero Snap will resize a window if you drag one side of a window to the edge of the screen.

4. **B.** The Quick Launch toolbar was removed from the taskbar in favor of pinned icons.

5. **A.** The ribbon-style menu in Windows Explorer enables the options to change depending on the type of device being explored.

6. **D.** Unlike Vista, gadgets in Windows 7 can appear anywhere on the desktop.

7. **D.** Right-clicking a program icon on the taskbar opens the Jump List.

8. **B.** Only folders can populate a library; files and printers have to sit this one out.

9. **C.** To reveal hidden files (or folders or drives), go to Organize | Folder and search options | View | Show hidden files, folders, and drives.

10. **C.** Windows 7 is most like Windows Vista. You could even call it Windows Vista 2, but no one would know what you were talking about.

CHAPTER 2

Installing Windows 7

This chapter ties into what you learned from

- **All-In-One:** Chapter 14
- **Managing and Troubleshooting:** Chapter 14
- **Meyers' Guide to 701:** Chapter 11

Windows 7 takes the good parts from Windows Vista and adds a few small items that make installation even easier. This chapter looks at three areas of difference between the two operating systems.

We'll begin by looking at the different editions of Windows 7 you'll see on the CompTIA A+ exams, including a list of important features in each version. The second section of the chapter walks through the preinstallation tasks in Windows 7, outlining the variations between 7 and Vista. The final section of the chapter details the changing landscape of hard drive structures that you need to understand to support installing Windows 7 on large hard drives and solid state drives. These technologies—UEFI, GPT, and BOOTMGR—do more than that, so I'll use this opportunity to go into them in some detail.

NOTE I won't repeat the actual steps for installing Windows 7 in this chapter. The original CompTIA A+ book covered the Windows Vista installation, and you'd need to squint to see the differences between that and the Windows 7 version.

Editions of Windows 7

You can bet that CompTIA will test you on the differences among the editions of Windows 7. Let's begin by listing the Windows 7 editions added to the 220-701 and 220-702 exams (Figure 2-1). They are:

- Windows 7 Starter
- Windows 7 Home Premium

Figure 2-1   Three of the four new editions of Windows 7 on the CompTIA A+ exams

- Windows 7 Professional
- Windows 7 Ultimate

Here, I've listed some important features and described which editions have which features. First, those features are:

- 64-bit edition available
- Aero Desktop
- Media Center
- Domain Login
- Encrypting File System (EFS)
- BitLocker Drive Encryption
- Windows XP Mode

 NOTE With the exception of the last item on the list, every item functions pretty much the same in Windows 7 as they do in Windows Vista, so no need to rehash them here.

The table below compares the features available in each edition of Windows 7. I strongly recommend you make it a point to memorize this table.

	64-bit Edition	Aero	Media Center	Join a Domain	EFS	BitLocker	Windows XP Mode
Windows 7 Starter	No	No	No	No	No	No	No
Windows 7 Home Premium	Yes	Yes	Yes	No	No	No	No
Windows 7 Professional	Yes	Yes	No	Yes	Yes	Yes	Yes
Windows 7 Ultimate	Yes	Yes	Yes	Yes	Yes	Yes	Yes

CompTIA did not add two other editions of Windows 7 to the CompTIA A+ exams: Home Basic and Enterprise. Microsoft created Windows 7 Home Basic exclusively for "emerging markets." This edition sits between Starter and Home Premium in terms of features. Large business and corporate customers can purchase Windows 7 Enterprise, a nonretail, highly customizable edition of Windows 7 sold through volume licensing.

EXAM TIP CompTIA references editions of Windows 7 not covered on the exams, such as Enterprise, in incorrect answers. Watch out!

Preinstallation Tasks

The CompTIA A+ exams define nine distinct preinstallation tasks for all versions of Windows. Let's look at each of these tasks and see how things have changed since Windows Vista. I've listed all nine steps here for quick reference:

1. Identify hardware requirements.
2. Verify hardware and software compatibility.
3. Decide what type of installation to perform.
4. Determine how to back up and restore existing data, if necessary.
5. Select an installation method.
6. Determine how to partition the hard drive and what file system to use.
7. Determine your computer's network role.
8. Decide on your computer's language and locale settings.
9. Plan for post-installation tasks.

Identify Hardware Requirements

Traditionally, Microsoft used a bewildering array of system requirements, making it unclear what hardware you needed to run a particular operating system. This happened because certain long-lived versions of Windows (mainly Windows XP) received many patches and grew tremendously, motivating Microsoft to update the hardware requirements. Of course, Microsoft never actually announced these new hardware requirements in any big way, making CompTIA A+ exam questions on system requirements a bit of a challenge in years past. Also, Microsoft released "minimum" and "recommended" hardware requirements, which made you wonder which one you should know for the CompTIA A+ exams (Figure 2-2).

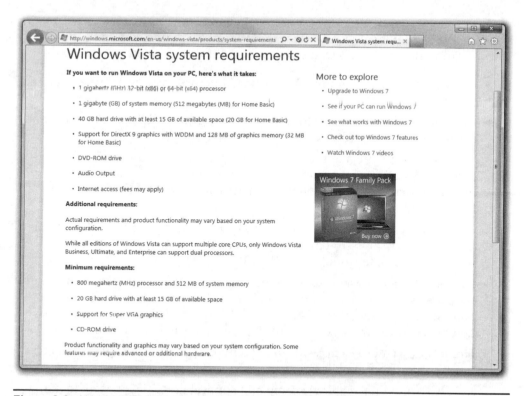

Figure 2-2 Windows Vista minimum and recommended requirements

Microsoft broke this tradition with Windows 7, releasing a single list of system requirements, broken down into 32-bit and 64-bit editions. Quoting directly from Microsoft's Windows 7 Web site:

- 1 gigahertz (GHz) or faster 32-bit (x86) or 64-bit (x64) processor
- 1 gigabyte (GB) RAM (32-bit) or 2 GB RAM (64-bit)
- 16 GB available hard disk space (32-bit) or 20 GB (64-bit)
- DirectX 9 graphics device with WDDM 1.0 or higher driver

NOTE Windows 7 has incredibly humble minimum requirements. Today, a low-end desktop computer will have 4 GB of RAM, a processor around 2 GHz, approximately a terabyte of hard drive space, and a DirectX 11 video card with 256 or even 512 MB of graphics memory.

Make sure you memorize the list of requirements. Microsoft also added a fairly extensive list of additional requirements that vary based on the edition of Windows 7 you use. From the same Web site, they include (author's comments in brackets):

- Internet access (fees may apply). [You need Internet access to activate, register, and update the system easily.]

- Depending on resolution, video playback may require additional memory and advanced graphics hardware.

- Some games and programs might require a graphics card compatible with DirectX 10 or higher for optimal performance. [Video has improved dramatically over the years and DirectX 9 dates back to 2004. Many games and high-definition videos need more than DirectX 9.]

- [Windows Aero Desktop (aka Aero Glass) adds amazing beauty and functionality to your Desktop. You must have a video card with 128 MB of graphics memory for Aero to work.]

- For some Windows Media Center functionality, a TV tuner and additional hardware may be required. [Windows Media Center works fine without a TV tuner. You can still use it to play Blu-ray Disc and DVD movies as well as video files and music. If you want to watch live TV, however, you'll need a tuner.]

- HomeGroup requires a network and PCs running Windows 7. [Read Chapter 6 for details on homegroups.]

- DVD/CD authoring requires a compatible optical drive. [If you want to burn something to an optical disc, you need a drive that can burn discs.]

- Windows XP Mode requires an additional 1 GB of RAM and an additional 15 GB of available hard disk space. [Windows 7 needs more system resources to power this mode.]

Windows 7 was also designed to handle multiple CPU cores and multiple CPUs. Many, if not most, modern computers use multicore processors. The 32-bit editions of Windows 7 can handle up to 32 processor cores, numbers that should make it an easy fact to remember for the exams. The 64-bit editions of Windows 7 support up to 256 processor cores.

In terms of multiple physical processors (found on high-end PCs), Windows 7 Professional and Ultimate can handle two CPUs, whereas Windows 7 Starter and Home Premium only support one CPU.

Verify Hardware and Software Compatibility

Previous versions of Windows provided a combination of Web sites and utilities that enabled you to verify both hardware and software compatibility on your system before you installed Windows. Windows 7 continues that tradition, including a new set of tools and sites to assist you.

Windows 7 uses the Windows 7 Compatibility Center Web site, formerly known as the Windows Logo'd Product List (for Windows Vista), the Windows Catalog (for Windows XP), and the Hardware Compatibility List (for Windows 2000 and XP). Now the magic words are Windows 7 Compatibility Center, as shown in Figure 2-3. Here you can find information on compatible components for your operating system.

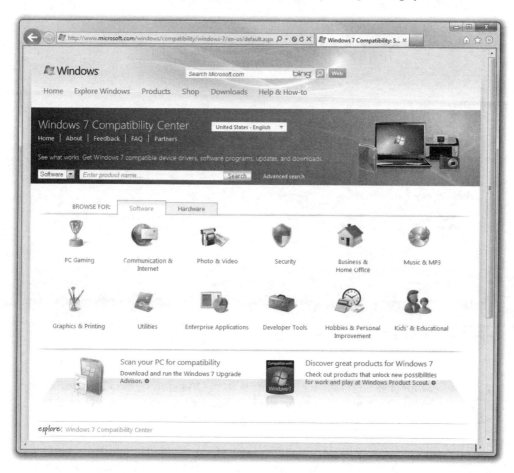

Figure 2-3   Windows 7 Compatibility Center

If you still use Windows Vista, you should download the Windows 7 Upgrade Advisor from the Windows 7 Compatibility Center. This tool scans your hardware, devices, and programs for known compatibility issues and offers solutions to get you ready for installing Windows 7 (Figure 2-4).

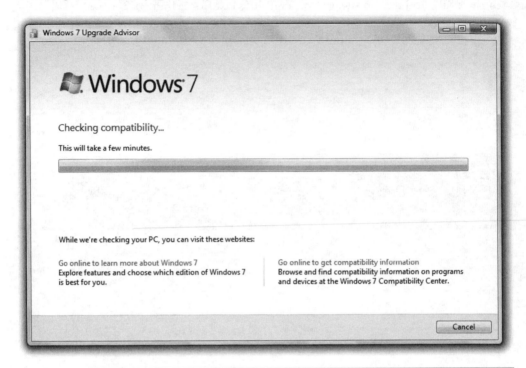

Figure 2-4   Windows 7 Upgrade Advisor

   EXAM TIP   Windows Vista came with the Windows Vista Upgrade Advisor, so when we're talking about the Upgrade Advisor in general, get used to simply saying the Windows OS Upgrade Advisor.

Before Windows 7, most Windows installation CDs or DVDs included a copy of the Windows OS Upgrade Advisor. This copy, however, quickly became dated as new technologies came along. Today, if you run SETUP.EXE on a Windows 7 installation DVD, you'll see the following screen (Figure 2-5).

Running *Check compatibility online* requires that you have an Internet connection because the installer will take you to the Windows 7 Compatibility Center Web site.

For folks looking to upgrade entire networks, Microsoft provides the far more powerful and complex Microsoft Assessment and Planning Toolkit (Figure 2-6). Unlike the Windows OS Upgrade Advisor, the Microsoft Assessment and Planning Toolkit queries an entire network, including the different operating systems, versions of Microsoft Office, and even SQL servers, and then tells you what you need to do to raise your network up to Windows 7 standards. This tool should not be used by those looking to upgrade one machine (or even a small network of systems).

Figure 2-5 Windows 7 installation screen

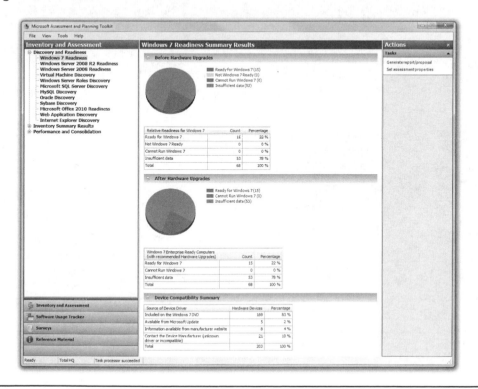

Figure 2-6 Microsoft Assessment and Planning Toolkit

Decide What Type of Installation to Perform

Windows 7 did not add anything new in terms of installation types. You still need to decide between a clean and an upgrade installation, but that's easy to do because you can only upgrade to Windows 7 from Windows Vista—and that's only if you have the same bit version. In other words, you can upgrade 32-bit Vista to 32-bit Windows 7, but you can't upgrade 32-bit Windows Vista to 64-bit Windows 7. All other Windows versions require a clean installation to get Windows 7.

If you have Windows 7 and you want to upgrade to a higher edition with more features, for example, from Windows 7 Home Premium to Windows 7 Ultimate, you can use the built-in Windows Anytime Upgrade feature. You can find this option pinned to the Start menu. Don't forget your credit card!

Determine How to Back Up and Restore Existing Data, If Necessary

Windows 7 doesn't take away the need for backups, but the same tools you learned about in the main text, including the Files and Settings Transfer Wizard (Windows XP) and Windows Easy Transfer (Windows Vista and 7), work exactly as they did before.

Select an Installation Method

The installation methods remain the same, as well. Use bootable installation media like a DVD to install Windows 7 on a single system. The Windows 7 installer handles more advanced installations, such as automated and network installations, just like Windows Vista.

You won't find many differences between the Windows Vista and Windows 7 installations (Figure 2-7). Only the splash screens and CD-key entry dialog box have changed! Because of this single, trivial difference, showing the installation process would waste paper.

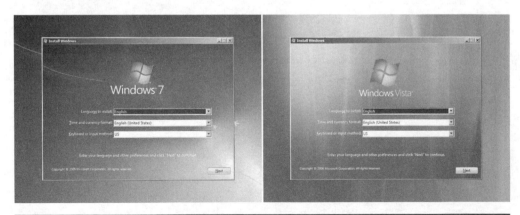

Figure 2-7 Windows 7 and Vista splash screens

Determine How to Partition the Hard Drive and What File System to Use

The vast majority of us want to use a single partition because it keeps things simple. Newer file system technologies, however, make this a bit of a challenge. To appreciate these changes, we need to have an entirely different discussion. Let's finish the preinstallation steps for now and then return to partitions and file systems later in the chapter.

Determine Your Computer's Network Role

You'll need to know if your computer connects to a workgroup or a domain. Some editions of Windows 7 add a new feature called HomeGroup, a new kind of workgroup that I'll discuss further in Chapter 6.

Decide on Your Computer's Language and Locale Settings and Plan for Post-Installation Tasks

Microsoft hasn't changed the Language and Locale Settings or other post-installation tasks in Windows 7. Refer to the main text to complete the installation job! Before you do that, however, you need to learn about some important changes taking place behind the scenes.

The Transition to UEFI, GPT, and BOOTMGR

Three technologies have converged to provide support for installing Windows on drives bigger than 2.2 TB. First, BIOS, as we know it, is gone, replaced by the *Unified Extensible Firmware Interface (UEFI)*. Second, the old MBR and partition tables are being replaced by a far more powerful technology called *GUID Partition Tables (GPT)*. Third, Windows Vista and Windows 7 have replaced the old NTLDR/NTDETECT/BOOT.INI with Windows Boot Manager, better known as BOOTMGR (often pronounced "boot mugger").

Let's take a look at all three of these changes.

EFI/UEFI

Your computer's system BIOS is one very old piece of programming. First conceived with the 286-based IBM AT computer back in the 1980s, BIOS hasn't changed much since then. As a result, BIOS only works in 16-bit mode and depends on x86-compliant hardware. In addition, if you had more than one OS loaded on a single drive, you needed one of those installed OSes to "take charge" and act as a boot loader. If computing was going to move forward, a new type of BIOS needed to come along. Intel's *Extensible Firmware Interface (EFI)* fills that role. In 2005, Intel released EFI for public standards, creating the Unified EFI forum to manage the specification. EFI was then renamed *Unified Extensible Firmware Interface (UEFI)*.

 TECH TIP   Even though it's really *UEFI*, most techs use the term *EFI*.

UEFI acts as a super-BIOS, doing the same job as BIOS but in a 64-bit environment. UEFI, though, does much more than just fill in for BIOS. Think of UEFI as a not yet extremely well-defined, industry-standard, mini–operating system that runs on top of the firmware of your computer, enabling you to do some pretty cool things at boot. Here are some of the things UEFI does:

- UEFI supports 32-bit or 64-bit booting.
- UEFI handles all boot-loading duties.
- UEFI is not dependent on x86 firmware.

UEFI became a standard years ago, so why did no one see a UEFI motherboard until 2011? The answer is simple: 3-TB hard drives. Regular BIOS does not support any type of volume other than master boot record drives, and MBR drives don't support partitions greater than 2.2 TB. As 3-TB and larger drives began to appear in 2011, people using traditional BIOS discovered that strange issues popped up when they wanted to boot off of a 3-TB hard drive (Figure 2-8). Instead of a 3-TB volume, you'd find a 2.2-TB volume and unpartitioned space.

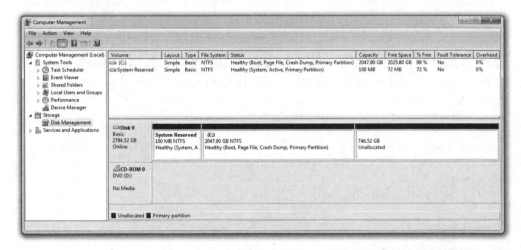

Figure 2-8 Here's what happens when you install Windows 7 on a greater-than 2.2-TB drive using regular BIOS.

UEFI motherboards support booting a newer type of hard-drive partitioning called *GUID Partition Table* (*GPT*). Although we'll discuss GPT in more detail shortly, understand for now that if you want to boot off of a hard drive using a single partition greater than 2.2 TB in Windows, you must use a UEFI motherboard and the hard drive must be blank. If your system meets these two criteria, the Windows 7 installation routine will automatically make a GPT drive for you (Figure 2-9).

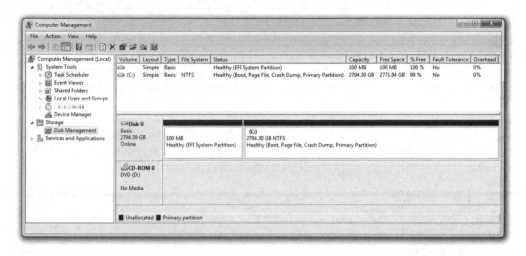

Figure 2-9 Here's what happens when you install Windows 7 on a greater-than 2.2-TB drive using UEFI.

 NOTE While UEFI works both for 32-bit and 64-bit operating systems, Microsoft decided to enable UEFI support only for 64-bit editions of Windows 7.

Although the EFI folks clearly defined issues such as booting and accessing firmware, they didn't define issues such as the graphical user interface or audio. If you think UEFI possesses a standard interface similar to the Windows desktop, forget it. UEFI serves as a non-hardware-specific, non-OS-specific, 32- or 64-bit bootloader. This doesn't make things we know and love such as POST or System Setup go away. They still exist, but now UEFI runs the show instead of BIOS (Figure 2-10).

Figure 2-10 POST and System Setup are still here.

The Adjustment Period

During the next few years, the industry will transition from BIOS to UEFI. Like any transition, weird and wacky things happen. For example, only Windows 64-bit supports UEFI. Microsoft most likely determined that by the time UEFI became dominant, only 64-bit systems would exist. Also, you can't determine if a motherboard is UEFI just by looking at it. Very few motherboards have a "Turn on UEFI" option in System Setup. Most are either UEFI *or* BIOS. Alternatively, some UEFI motherboards currently have the ability to "fall back" to BIOS if you're not running 64-bit Windows 7, making it rather tricky to determine if your motherboard is UEFI or not. For now, the best place to verify UEFI-status is with good old Web research (Figure 2-11).

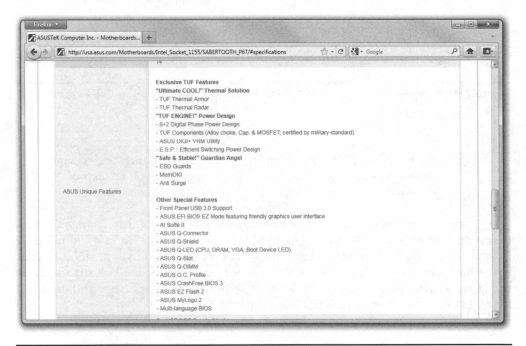

Figure 2-11 Web research showing a motherboard is UEFI

From a tech's standpoint, UEFI doesn't really change how you "see" the BIOS. You'll still see a POST, and you'll still press F2 or DEL to access System Setup. Just like BIOS, you access the boot order in System Setup.

Once you're in System Setup, however, you might see a big change. With UEFI, System Setup utilities can easily use GUIs and each BIOS maker/motherboard manufacturer creates their own interface. Figure 2-12 shows a graphical UEFI-based ASUS System Setup. Figure 2-13 shows the boot order in a UEFI System Setup.

Figure 2-12   System Setup

Figure 2-13   Boot order in a UEFI System Setup

   NOTE   UEFI motherboards don't have to use graphical System Setup utilities, but most do.

EFI System Partitions

The big change with UEFI isn't how it displays the boot options, but where it stores the boot data. On all operating systems using UEFI, the boot drive needs a small partition just for UEFI system files. For Windows, this partition is usually around 100 MB. Microsoft calls this partition the *EFI System Partition*.

An EFI System Partition holds the boot information for all the different operating systems on the computer. Windows calls this boot information the *Boot Configuration Data* (*BCD*), which is analogous to the old BOOT.INI file. The downside is that, unlike the easy-to-read BOOT.INI text file, the BCD stored in the EFI System Partition is not easily accessible. To work with the BCD, you'll need BCDEDIT, which I'll cover in Chapter 3.

The End of MBR

While UEFI gets rid of the last of the 16-bit code on your motherboard, there's one place where 16-bit code still resides on your hard drive: the master boot record and partition table. Since the first hard drives were installed in PCs, we've used the ancient master boot record and partition table, collectively called *MBR drives*, to organize and store data. Let's quickly review MBR drives and then add a little more detail to what you already know.

The first sector on all hard drives is known as the boot sector, partition sector, or even the master boot record. This sector consists of two critical data structures: the boot code (also called the master boot record—yes, two different things get the same name, sorry) and the partition table (Figure 2-14).

NOTE I, Mike Meyers, have been calling the first sector on your hard drive the *boot sector* for over 20 years. From now on, I will call the first sector the *partition boot sector*. I will call the first sector on every partition the *boot sector*.

Figure 2-14
MBR in detail

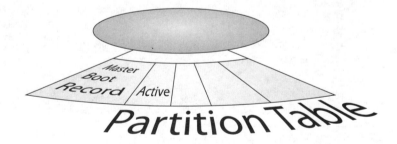

MBR is already described in the different versions of the CompTIA A+ book, but to review: you cannot have more than four primary partitions, and the partition sector loads the initial boot code and then reads which of the four primary partitions is set to Active.

To add to Figure 2-14, let's now move to the first sector in any of the primary partitions. This is what we'll call the boot sector (Figure 2-15). The boot sector knows just enough to read the file system of this partition and find the location of the operating system's boot program.

Figure 2-15
Boot sector in detail

To make this easier to remember: a single drive will have a single *partition boot sector* but could have more than one *boot sector*.

 NOTE When you run FIXBOOT, you are actually fixing the boot sector on the bootable Windows primary partition. When you run FIXMBR you are repairing the boot code in the partition boot sector.

GUID Partition Tables

The old MBR-style of hard drive organization has three big problems. First, the boot code runs in 16-bit mode. Second, the partition tables don't support more than four primary partitions. Third, because of the way data is stored in each partition table entry, a single partition cannot be greater than 2.2 TB. Considering the fact that MBR was first invented in the early 1980s, it's impressive how long it lasted. But all good things must come to an end. That's why the UEFI standard includes a replacement for MBR called *GUID Partition Tables* (*GPT*).

As you might imagine, GPT fixes the problems inherent to MBR. Figure 2-16 shows a simplified diagram of a GPT. Note that GPT drives still provide a protective MBR. Inside this "fake" MBR is code identifying the drive as GPT. This is mainly to make bootable media aware that the drive is GPT.

Figure 2-16
GPT protective MBR

> **NOTE** GPT drives also support a legacy MBR instead of a protective MBR if you want the first partition on a drive to boot as an MBR drive.

Before we move on to other cool parts of GPT, let's cover a few important points:

- GPT loves logical block addressing (LBA). When LBA was invented back in 1990, the MBR was tweaked to "lie" to BIOS to make LBA look like the old cylinder-head-sector (CHS) values. With GPT, the lie is over. The protective MBR starts at LBA 0 and goes through every single logical block until you get to the end of the drive.

- GPT makes a backup of itself. A complete copy of the entire GPT is made at the end of the drive.

- GPT doesn't define a limit to the number of partitions, though Microsoft sets Windows to allow a maximum of 128 partitions.

- Every partition is identified with a *globally unique identifier* (*GUID*). A GUID is 128-bit identifier used in all kinds of ways in Windows. They look like this:

  {5A2C0411-AFF3-41D3-A90C-3051E82C3EA1}

- GPT supports drives with up to 2^{64} sectors.

Figure 2-17 shows a detailed view of GPT on a drive.

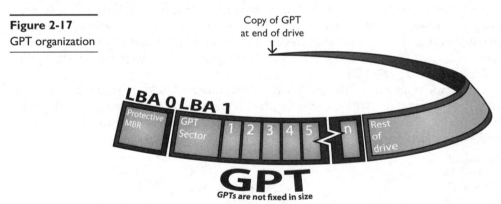

Figure 2-17
GPT organization

If you'd like to see a GPT drive in action, but you don't have a UEFI motherboard, no worries! Windows 7 completely supports GPT on BIOS motherboards, but only on drives that don't contain the Windows boot partition. So go grab an extra hard drive and add it to your Windows 7 system. Open Disk Management, select the drive you just added, right-click the drive type, and choose *Convert to GPT Disk*, as shown in Figure 2-18.

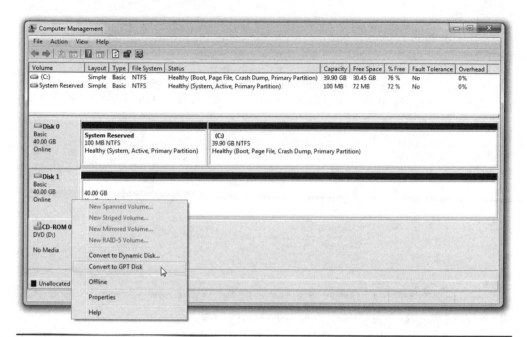

Figure 2-18   Converting a second drive to GPT

Once the drive is converted to GPT, you can make as many simple volumes as you wish. It does not matter if the disk is basic or dynamic—GPT gets you past the four partition limit. Keep in mind that unlike Windows XP, Windows Vista and Windows 7 call all partitions "volumes" whether they are on a basic drive or a dynamic drive. This has nothing to do with whether the drive is GPT or MBR; it's just Microsoft's way of (confusingly) doing things.

I know what you're thinking: doesn't Windows enable me to make more than four volumes using dynamic disks? If dynamic disks got us past the four partition limit, why even bother with GPT disks? There are a couple of very good reasons:

- GPT is an open industry standard. Dynamic disks are proprietary to Microsoft and no one knows exactly how they work.

- Dynamic disks still lean on the MBR concept and, as a result, are limited to 2.2 TB partitions in non-RAID drives.

   NOTE   GPT drives can either be basic or dynamic disks.

Nothing stops you from making GPT disks dynamic, but would you? Many techs skip dynamic drives and use basic ones instead. If you want to use RAID, use hardware RAID.

If you want to shrink or grow volumes, you can do that with (Vista's and 7's) basic disks. If you want to span two drives, well, then you need to use dynamic disks.

You know that a basic disk uses primary, extended, or logical partitions, and a dynamic disk uses volumes. This is true with Windows XP, but Microsoft obscures this in Vista and 7: both basic and dynamic drives use "volumes." Figure 2-19 shows a basic GPT drive with four simple volumes. Compare this figure with Figure 2-20, a hard drive kept as an MBR drive.

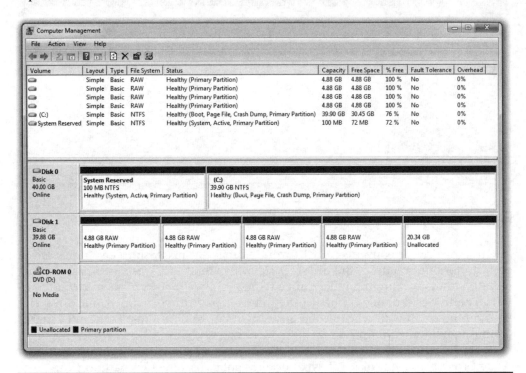

Figure 2-19   GPT drive with many simple volumes

In keeping with MBR's four-partition limit, creating a fourth simple volume reveals a surprising fact. These aren't simple volumes at all (even if that's what Windows Vista and Windows 7 call them)—they're three classic primary partitions, and Windows automatically makes the fourth partition an extended partition.

GPT, being a part of the UEFI standard, has been around for years. All Intel-based Macs have UEFI and use GPT drives. Linux systems support UEFI and GPT, although a lack of motherboards until mid-2011 prevented heavy GPT adoption. To make these technologies mainstream, Microsoft Windows needed to step up to the plate and support them. But to do it, Windows needed to dump the old NTLDR world and come up with something new.

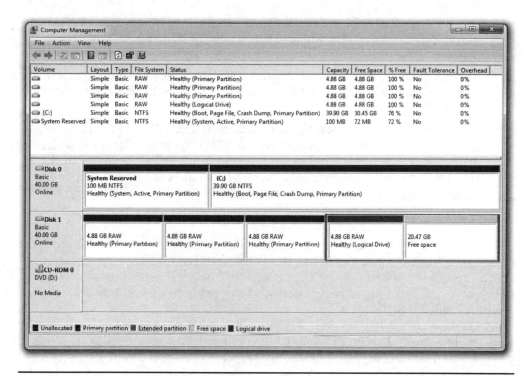

Figure 2-20 MBR drive with four partitions

BOOTMGR

Since the design of Windows NT in the early 1990s, the Windows boot sequence, using a standard BIOS and an MBR drive, went something like this (Figure 2-21):

1. BIOS inspects the set boot order and goes to the first drive in the list.

2. The MBR runs, inspecting the partition table for an active partition.

3. The system is directed to the boot sector of the active partition, reads the code in that sector, which directs it, in turn, to the operating system boot file. The primary boot file for Windows was NTLDR.

Figure 2-21
Old school boot

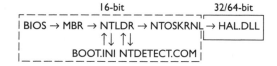

4. NTDLR looks for BOOT.INI which must be in the same folder as itself. The BOOT.INI file tells NTLDR where to find a copy of Windows to load into memory.

5. After reading the BOOT.INI, NTLDR loads NTDETECT.COM to verify that the copy of Windows described in BOOT.INI has enough of the critical pieces to (hopefully) start.

6. At this point NTLDR fires up NTOSKRNL.EXE and HAL.DLL. NTOSKRNL is the actual "main piece," "core," or "kernel" of Windows and, most importantly, the first part that moves Windows from 16-bit mode into 32- or 64-bit mode. HAL.DLL acts as the interface between all of the hardware on your system and Windows.

7. After this, other critical files load and you eventually get to your Desktop.

This system worked perfectly up through Windows XP. After that, however, Windows had a big problem. Microsoft knew that UEFI/GPT would eventually become "the thing," but the BIOS/MBR system was still widely used. To support both worlds, Microsoft had to invent a new way to load Windows that supported both the old way and the new way. They called it BOOTMGR.

BOOTMGR completely replaces NTLDR in Windows Vista and 7. NTLDR doesn't work in these newer versions of Windows. If you install Windows Vista or Windows 7, you use BOOTMGR. Let's go through the boot process again, this time replacing NTLDR with BOOTMGR.

1. BIOS inspects the set boot order and goes to the first drive in the list.

2. The MBR runs, inspecting the partition table for an active partition.

3. The system is directed to the boot sector of the active partition, reads the code in that sector, which directs it, in turn, to the operating system boot file. The primary boot file for Windows is BOOTMGR.

At this point, the boot process in Vista and 7 differ a lot:

1. In Vista, BOOTMGR sits in the root directory of the boot drive, as shown in Figure 2-22.

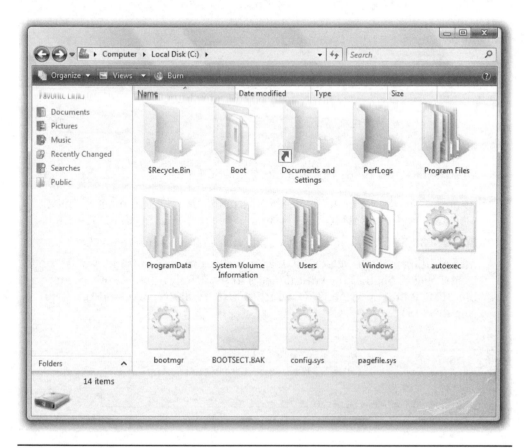

Figure 2-22 BOOTMGR in Windows Vista

2. BOOTMGR looks for a special data store called the BCD store. Unless you are using UEFI, the BCD information is always stored in the boot drive in the \BOOT\BCD folder.

3. After reading the BCD, BOOTMGR verifies that the copy of Windows described in BCD has enough of the critical pieces to (hopefully) start. At this point BOOTMGR fires up WINLOAD, which, in turn, starts NTOSKRNL.EXE and HAL.DLL (Figure 2-23).

Figure 2-23
Vista boot
process

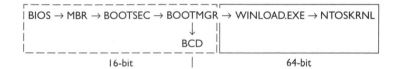

The Windows 7 boot process is very similar to Vista with one exception: BOOTMGR sits in its own special reserved partition, as seen in Figure 2-24.

Figure 2-24
Windows 7 boot process

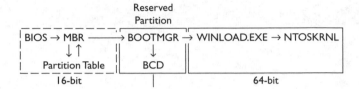

If you switch to UEFI on 64-bit Windows 7, the boot process changes even more:

1. UEFI inspects the set boot order and goes to the first drive in the list, called BOOTMGR.EFI. BOOTMGR.EFI is simply the UEFI version of BOOTMGR.

2. BOOTMGR.EFI runs, inspecting the EFI system partition for the BCD.

3. After reading the BCD, BOOTMGR verifies that the copy of Windows described in BCD has enough of the critical pieces to (hopefully) start. At this point BOOTMGR fires up WINLOAD, which starts NTOSKRNL.EXE and HAL.DLL (Figure 2-25).

Figure 2-25
UEFI Windows 7 boot

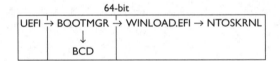

Implementing UEFI and GPT in Windows Vista and Windows 7

The world is quickly moving from BIOS motherboards reading MBR drives using Windows XP's NTLDR to a new world where UEFI boots up GPT drives that use Windows Vista's and Windows 7's BOOTMGR.

The next time you install Windows, you might not even notice this transition, especially if you have current hardware and software:

- A UEFI motherboard
- A blank hard drive
- Installation media for 64-bit Windows 7

The Windows installation detects UEFI drives and automatically configures and installs itself on a GPT drive. Let's take a look at the results and compare these to an older installation routine using BIOS/MBR.

The System Reserved/EFI System Partition

Except for a few unique situations, all Windows 7 installations try to create roughly a 100 MB partition at the beginning of the bootable drive. This partition goes by two names: on most systems using standard BIOS and MBR boots, Disk Management calls this the *System Reserved partition*. On UEFI systems, as you saw earlier in the chapter, it is called the EFI System Partition. It is not assigned a drive letter, is always a primary partition and is always set as active. A few points:

- All editions of Windows 7 will try to make this partition. As long as you are installing to a blank drive, it will create this partition.
- This partition should never be uninstalled.
- It is *not* just for UEFI/GPT.
- It does not require a dynamic disk.
- It supports any file system, but why use anything other than NTFS?

Figure 2-26 shows the Disk Management results of installing 32-bit Windows 7 Ultimate onto a 1-TB hard drive on a BIOS motherboard. Note the System Reserved partition is shown as active.

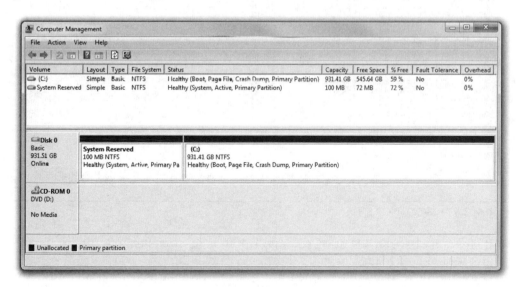

Figure 2-26   System Reserved partition

In a BIOS/MBR installation, the System Reserved partition stores BOOTMGR, a backup copy of the BCD, and, if installed, critical information for BitLocker Drive Encryption.

Inspecting a Windows UEFI/GPT Installation

The EFI System Partition holds BOOTMGR.EFI, the UEFI version of BOOTMGR you see on BIOS-based Windows Vista/7 systems. Figure 2-27 shows the BOOTMGR.EFI file stored on the EFI System Partition. To see the EFI System Partition, I used the MOUNTVOL Z: /s command.

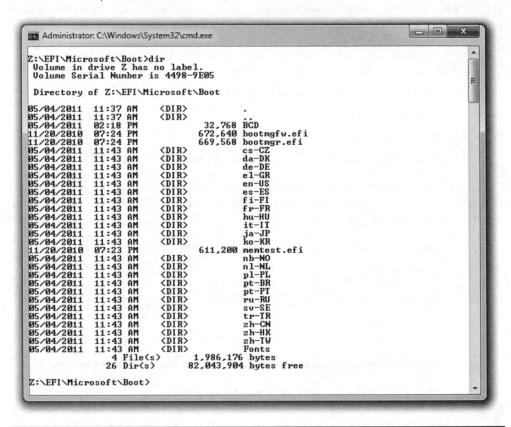

Figure 2-27 BOOTMGR.EFI

If you don't have a UEFI drive, you may still look in the system partition using the Mount tool in Disk Management, as shown in Figure 2-28.

Once the drive is mounted, open a command prompt as a local administrator and locate the BOOTMGR (no extension) file. Be sure to go into Folder Options in a Windows Explorer window, check the *Show hidden files, folders, and drives* option and uncheck the *Hide protected operating system files* option. You should see the BOOTMGR file as shown in Figure 2-29.

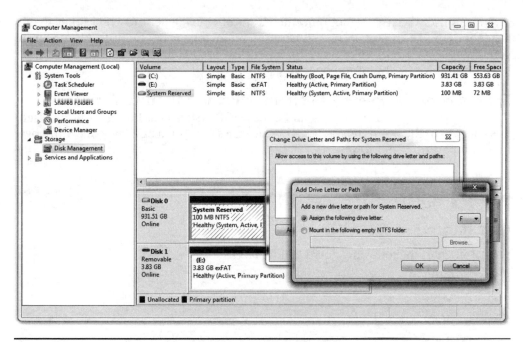

Figure 2-28 Mounting the system partition on a non-EFI system

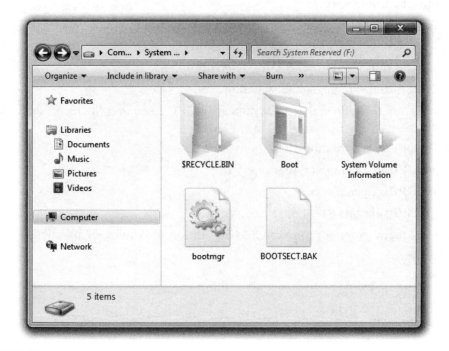

Figure 2-29 BOOTMGR

From a user or tech's standpoint, there's no obvious benefit to UEFI other than a faster boot up. The power of UEFI comes from removing the last bit of 16-bit code from your computer and creating a powerful, extensible pre-OS framework that matches the power of today's hardware and operating systems.

They May Be Completely Different—But Get Used to Them!

Wow! The onslaught of UEFI, GPT, and BOOTMGR systems has brought on some serious changes in the way techs see PCs. These features give you a new level of control over how you partition your drives.

Chapter Review

Questions

1. Which of the following does UEFI replace?

   A. GPT

   B. MBR

   C. BOOTMGR

   D. BIOS

2. To create a GPT drive during a Windows 7 installation, which of the following must be true? (Select two.)

   A. The hard drive must be blank.

   B. You must be using a UEFI motherboard.

   C. You must use BitLocker Drive Encryption.

   D. It must be an upgrade installation.

3. Which of the following is an advantage of GPT drives over Microsoft's dynamic disks?

   A. GPT allows for more than four volumes.

   B. GPT uses a graphical user interface.

   C. GPT is open source.

   D. GPT supports 64-bit operating systems.

4. How many processor cores can a 64-bit edition of Windows 7 handle?

   A. 1

   B. 8

   C. 128

   D. 256

5. How can you best determine that your motherboard uses UEFI, not BIOS?

   A. Physically inspect the board.

   B. Check the System Setup utility.

   C. Check the System applet in Control Panel.

   D. Look up information about the board on the Internet.

6. Which of the following editions of Windows 7 are not covered on the CompTIA A+ exams? (Select two.)

   A. Windows 7 Home Basic

   B. Windows 7 Home Premium

   C. Windows 7 Ultimate Edition

   D. Windows 7 Enterprise

7. Windows XP creates partitions on basic disks. In Windows 7, what are these called?

   A. Partitions

   B. Volumes

   C. Tables

   D. Drives

8. Where does the final piece of 16-bit code reside on a Windows machine?

   A. GUID partition table

   B. MBR partition table

   C. BIOS

   D. UEFI

9. How much hard drive space does the 32-bit edition of Windows 7 require?

   A. 12 GB

   B. 13 GB

   C. 16 GB

   D. 20 GB

10. What is the file name for the EFI version of BOOTMGR?

   A. BOOTMGREFI

   B. BOOT.EFI

   C. BOOTMGREFI.EFI

   D. BOOTMGR.EFI

Answers

1. **D.** UEFI replaces the BIOS.

2. **A, B.** Creating a GPT drive during Windows 7's installation requires a UEFI motherboard and a blank hard drive.

3. **C.** GPT is open source, whereas Microsoft's dynamic disks use a proprietary technology.

4. **D.** The 64-bit edition of Windows 7 can handle up to 256 processor cores.

5. **D.** The best way to determine if your motherboard uses UEFI is to look it up online.

6. **A, D.** Windows 7 Home Basic and Windows 7 Enterprise are not covered on the current CompTIA A+ exams.

7. **B.** Even on basic disks, Windows creates what it calls "volumes" (even though they are really partitions).

8. **B.** The last bits of 16-bit code on a Windows PC can be found in the MBR partition table.

9. **C.** The 32-bit edition of Windows 7 needs 16 GB of available hard drive space.

10. **D.** The EFI version of BOOTMGR is (helpfully) called BOOTMGR.EFI.

CHAPTER 3

Boot Issues with Windows 7

This chapter ties into what you learned from

- **All-In-One:** Chapter 17
- **Managing and Troubleshooting:** Chapter 17
- **Meyers' Guide to 702:** Chapter 8

In the days before Windows Vista and Windows 7, we counted on Windows XP's recovery console to repair boot problems. Tools such as FIXBOOT and FIXMBR made quick work of broken systems in Windows XP. Microsoft introduced new tools in Windows Vista and Windows 7 to complement the advances in the boot process those operating systems made over previous versions.

This chapter covers everything you need to know about boot repair in Windows 7. I'll discuss each tool available in the Windows Recovery Environment, including Startup Repair, System Restore, and the Windows Memory Diagnostic Tool. You'll also learn more about the command prompt and some special commands available only in the Windows Recovery Environment.

WinPE and the Death of Recovery Console

Windows kept a dirty little secret for years. When you installed Windows from the bootable installation media (usually a CD or DVD), it actually booted up a copy of the ancient DOS operating system. You never saw DOS because an installation screen covered it up, but it lurked beneath the surface (Figure 3-1).

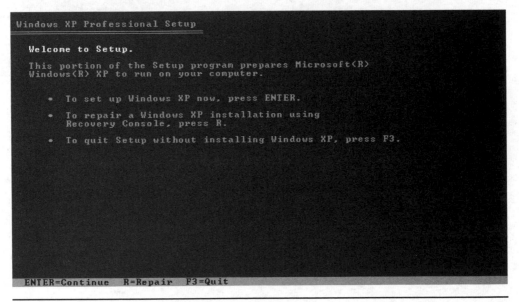

Figure 3-1 Windows XP install screen—it's really DOS.

With later versions of Windows XP and certainly with Windows Vista and Windows 7, Microsoft upgraded the installation environment from 16-bit to 32- and 64-bit. This upgrade enabled the Windows installation process to go graphical and support features such as a mouse pointer and clickable elements, rather than relying on command-line tools. Microsoft calls the installation environment the *Windows Preinstallation Environment*, shortened to *Windows PE or WinPE*.

With Windows PE, you can boot directly to the Windows CD or DVD. This loads a limited-function graphical operating system that contains both troubleshooting and diagnostic tools, along with installation options. The Windows installation media is called a *Live CD* or *Live DVD* because the WinPE loads directly from the disc into memory and doesn't access or modify the hard drive.

NOTE   Although here I discuss only how WinPE helps boot repair, know that WinPE goes much further. WinPE can assist unattended installations, network installations, and even booting diskless workstations on a network.

When you access Windows PE and opt for the troubleshooting and repair features, you open a special set of tools called the *Windows Recovery Environment*. Like with Windows PE, techs shorten this term to *Windows RE* or *WinRE*.

The terms can get a little confusing because of the similarity of letters, so mark this: Windows RE is the repair tools that run within the Windows PE. WinPE powers WinRE. Got it? Let's tackle WinRE.

EXAM TIP   CompTIA refers to the Windows Recovery Environment as the *System Recovery Options menu*.

Getting To and Using Windows RE

It would be unfair to say that the Windows Recovery Environment only replaces the old recovery console. WinRE includes an impressive, powerful set of both automated and manual utilities that collectively diagnose and fix all but the most serious of Windows boot problems. Although it does all the hard work for you, you still need to know how to access and use it.

Getting to Windows RE

In Windows 7, you can access WinRE in three ways. First, you can boot from your original installation media and select *Repair*. Second, you can use the *Repair Your Computer* option on the Advanced Boot Options (F8) menu (Figure 3-2). Third, you can create a system repair disc before you have problems. Go to **Control Panel | System and Security | Backup and Restore** and select *Create a system repair disc*, as shown in Figure 3-3.

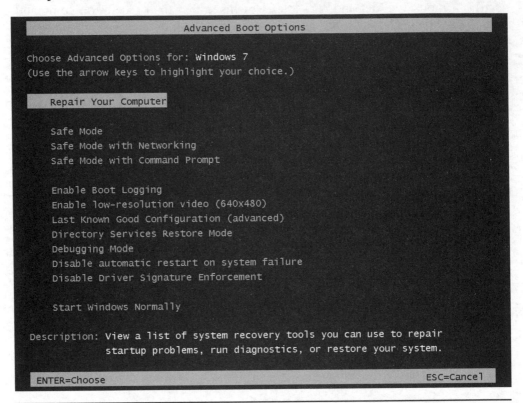

```
                     Advanced Boot Options

Choose Advanced Options for: Windows 7
(Use the arrow keys to highlight your choice.)


  Repair Your Computer


  Safe Mode
  Safe Mode with Networking
  Safe Mode with Command Prompt

  Enable Boot Logging
  Enable low-resolution video (640x480)
  Last Known Good Configuration (advanced)
  Directory Services Restore Mode
  Debugging Mode
  Disable automatic restart on system failure
  Disable Driver Signature Enforcement


  Start Windows Normally


Description: View a list of system recovery tools you can use to repair
            startup problems, run diagnostics, or restore your system.


ENTER=Choose                                              ESC=Cancel
```

Figure 3-2   Selecting Repair Your Computer in the Advanced Boot Options menu.

EXAM TIP   Windows Vista does not have the Repair Your Computer option on the Advanced Boot Options menu. You can either use your installation media or, if you have SP1 or later, make a bootable system repair disc.

Although any of these methods works fine, I recommend that you access WinRE from the installation media for three reasons:

1. Your hard drive can be so messed up that you won't make it to the Advanced Boot Options menu.

2. Accessing WinRE using the Repair Your Computer option in the Advanced Boot Options menu also requires a local administrator password.

3. Using a bootable disc enables you to avoid any malware that might be on your system.

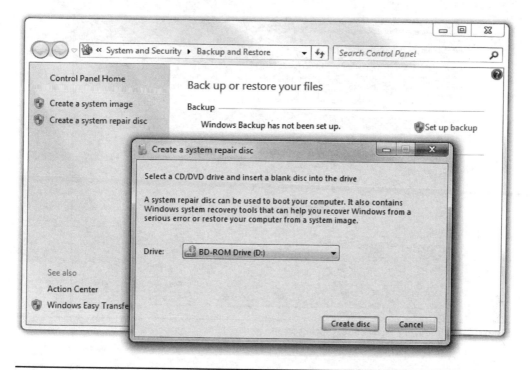

Figure 3-3   Making a system repair disc in Windows 7

Using Windows RE

No matter how you choose to access the Windows Recovery Environment, the main menu looks the same (Figure 3-4). You have five options in WinRE:

1. Startup Repair

2. System Restore

3. System Image Recovery or Windows Complete PC Restore

4. Windows Memory Diagnostic

5. Command Prompt

Option number three differs between Windows 7 and Windows Vista, though the intent—rebuilding from a backup—is the same. I'll talk about how these options differ a little later in the chapter.

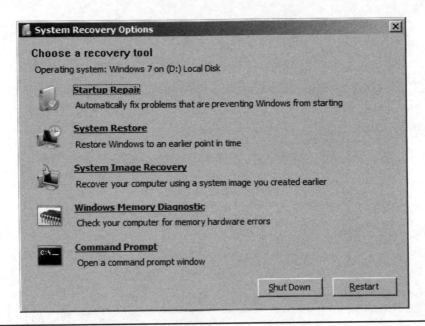

Figure 3-4   Recovery Environment main screen

 EXAM TIP   Make sure you know how to access the Windows Recovery Environment and what each of the available tools do.

Startup Repair

The Startup Repair utility serves as a one-stop, do-it-all option (Figure 3-5). When run, it performs a number of repairs, including:

- Repairs a corrupted registry by accessing the backup copy on your hard drive
- Restores critical system and driver files
- Runs the equivalent of the recovery console's FIXBOOT and FIXMBR
- Rolls back any nonworking drivers
- Uninstalls any incompatible service packs and patches
- Runs CHKDSK
- Runs a memory test to check your RAM

Startup Repair fixes almost any Windows boot problem. In fact, if you have a system with one hard drive containing a single partition with Windows Vista or Windows 7 installed, you'd have trouble finding something it *couldn't* fix. Upon completion, Startup Repair shows the screen seen in Figure 3-6.

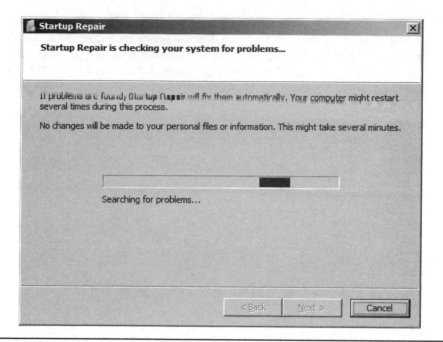

Figure 3-5   Startup Repair in action

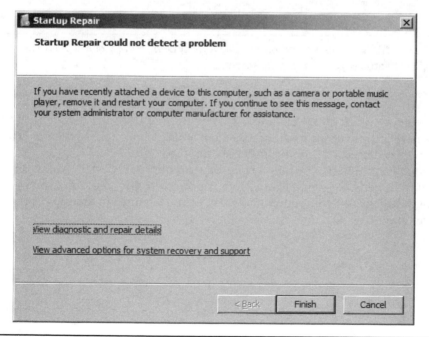

Figure 3-6   Startup Repair complete; no problems found.

Note the link in Figure 3-6 that says *View diagnostic and repair details*. This opens a text file called **SRTTRAIL.TXT** that lists exactly what the program found, what it fixed, and what it failed to do. It may look cryptic, but you can type anything you find into Google for more information. I've reproduced the beginning of the (very long) SRTTRAIL.TXT file here:

```
Startup Repair diagnosis and repair log
---------------------------
Last successful boot time: 12/14/2011 2:37:43 AM (GMT)
Number of repair attempts: 6

Session details
---------------------------
System Disk = \Device\Harddisk0
Windows directory = C:\Windows
AutoChk Run = 0
Number of root causes = 1

Test Performed:
---------------------------
Name: Check for updates
Result: Completed successfully. Error code =  0x0
Time taken = 32 ms

Test Performed:
---------------------------
Name: System disk test
Result: Completed successfully. Error code =  0x0
Time taken = 0 ms
```

 NOTE The *View advanced options for system recovery and support* link simply returns you to the main screen.

In Windows 7, Startup Repair starts automatically if your system detects a boot problem. If you fire up your Windows system and see the screen shown in Figure 3-7, Windows has detected a problem in the startup process.

Personally, I think this menu pops up way too often. If you fail to shut down your computer properly, for example, this menu appears. In this case, you can save time by booting normally. When in doubt, however, go ahead and run Startup Repair. It can't hurt anything.

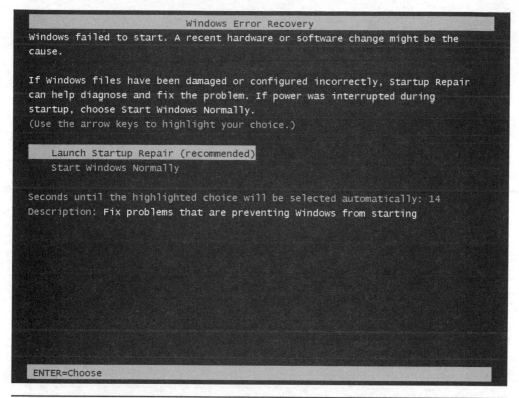

```
                        Windows Error Recovery
Windows failed to start. A recent hardware or software change might be the
cause.

If Windows files have been damaged or configured incorrectly, Startup Repair
can help diagnose and fix the problem. If power was interrupted during
startup, choose Start Windows Normally.
(Use the arrow keys to highlight your choice.)


    Launch Startup Repair (recommended)
    Start Windows Normally


Seconds until the highlighted choice will be selected automatically: 14
Description: Fix problems that are preventing Windows from starting




ENTER=Choose
```

Figure 3-7 Windows Error Recovery

A powerful tool like Startup Repair still doesn't cover everything. You may have specific needs that require more finesse than a single, do-it-all approach. In many cases, you've already discovered the problem and simply want to make a single fix. You might want to perform a system restoration or check the memory. For this, we'll need to explore the other four options available in WinRE.

 EXAM TIP If you have trouble booting your computer, you should try Startup Repair first.

System Restore
System Restore does the same job here it has done since Microsoft first introduced it in Windows Me. Placing this option in Windows RE gives those of us who make many restore points a quick and handy way to return our systems to a previous state (Figure 3-8).

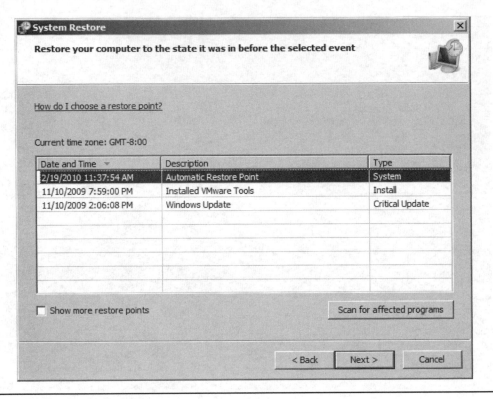

Figure 3-8 System Restore points

System Image Recovery/Windows Complete Restore

Windows 7's backup tools differ from Windows Vista's. Note Figure 3-9, which shows the Windows Vista Recovery Environment menu on the left next to the Windows 7 Recovery Environment on the right. The third WinRE option differs. Windows Vista uses the Windows Complete PC Restore utility, whereas Windows 7 includes the System Image Recovery tool.

To appreciate the different options, you must first know backup options in Windows Vista and Windows 7. These two operating systems truly changed the idea of system backup. Microsoft retired NTBackup with Windows XP, replacing it with the more automated and simpler *Backup and Restore Center* (Vista) and *Backup and Restore* (Windows 7) Control Panel applets. NTBackup required you to choose the files you wanted to back up as well as the type of backup (incremental, differential, or normal). Windows Vista and Windows 7 no longer ask those questions, at least not directly. In Windows Vista, you can either back up files or back up your computer (Figure 3-10). Both choices will first ask you where you want to store the backup (Figure 3-11).

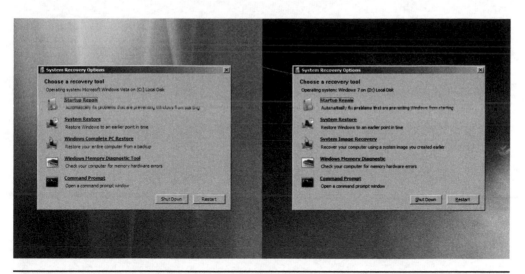

Figure 3-9   The WinRE options in Windows Vista and Windows 7

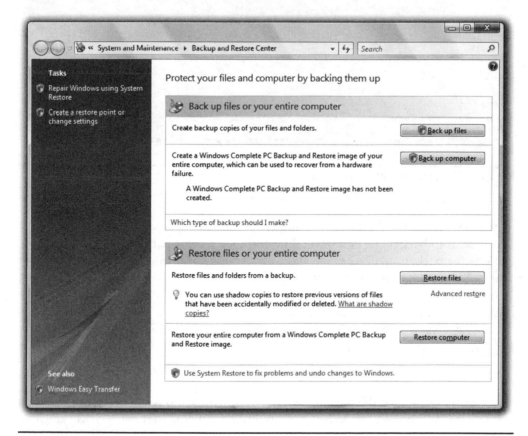

Figure 3-10   Backup options in Vista

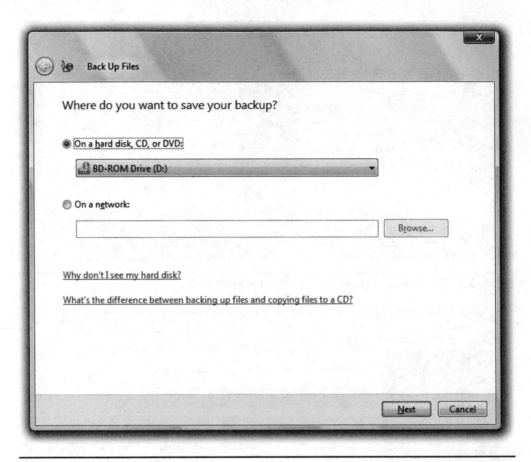

Figure 3-11   Backup location in Vista

Unlike NTBackup, Windows Vista and Windows 7 don't support backing up to tape. If you want to back up to tapes, you'll need to buy a third-party program. Acceptable options for backup media include flash drives, optical discs of all sorts, or you can make a backup over a network. You can even copy the backup to any hard drive, as long as it's not the drive you're backing up.

NOTE   Windows Vista and Windows 7 do not back up to tape drives.

As the name implies, the *Back up computer* option backs up your entire computer to a system image. Choosing the *Back up files* option is another matter entirely. Clicking this button doesn't bring up a directory tree like you saw in NTBackup. Instead, you see the screen shown in Figure 3-12.

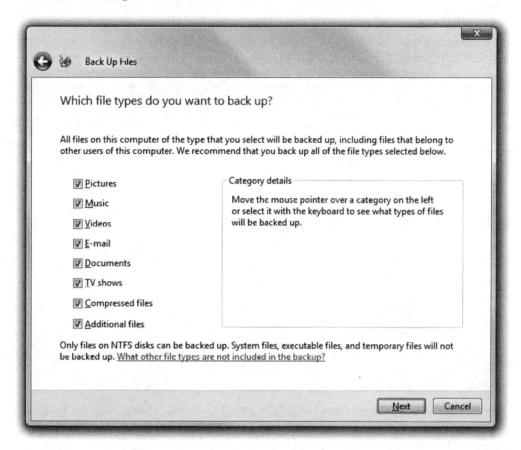

Figure 3-12 Types of files to back up

The *Back up files* option in Vista only enables you to back up personal information for all users. If you want to back up any installed applications, or even Windows itself, don't bother using the *Back up files* option that comes with Windows Vista.

EXAM TIP Windows Vista and Windows 7 will not back up content stored on non-NTFS volumes.

Windows 7's Backup and Restore utility includes a number of noteworthy improvements over Windows Vista's. First of all, Microsoft changed the look of the main screen (Figure 3-13).

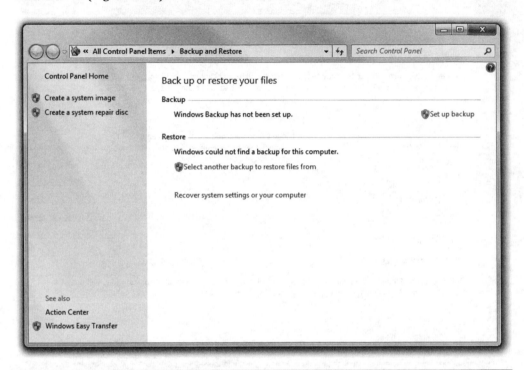

Figure 3-13 Windows 7 Backup and Restore

Clicking the *Set up backup* link in Windows 7 opens a dialog box asking you to choose your backup location—very similar to Vista's backup. After selecting your backup location and clicking *Next*, you then see the screen shown in Figure 3-14.

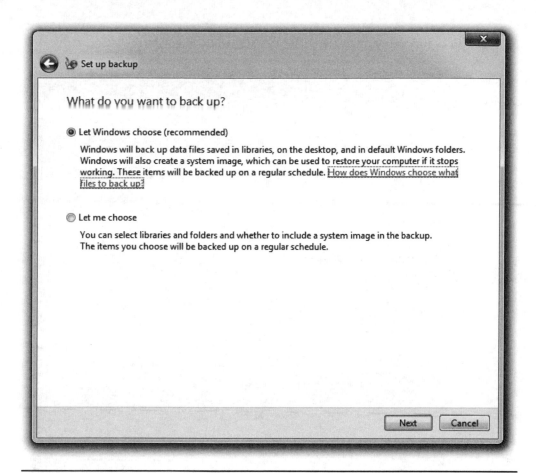

Figure 3-14 What do you want to back up?

If you select *Let Windows choose (recommended)*, you'll get a backup similar to the Vista backup, but with one very important difference. You'll back up each user's personal data, but Windows 7 doesn't stop there. Assuming you have enough space in your backup location, Windows 7 will automatically add a system image that includes the entire Windows operating system, every installed program, all device drivers, and even the registry.

NOTE   Windows image files use the .WIM extension.

Selecting *Let me choose* is equally interesting. Unlike Vista's selection, Windows 7 enables you to pick individual users' files to back up (Figure 3-15).

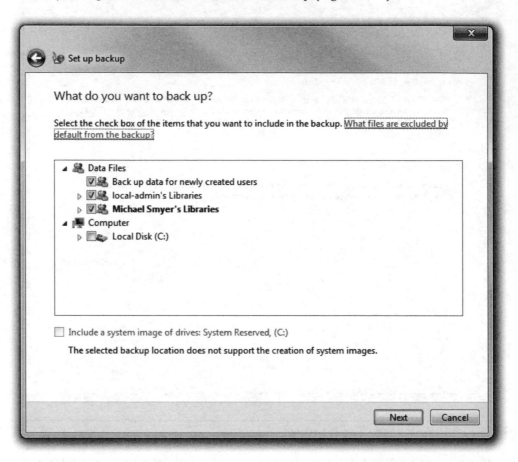

Figure 3-15   Backup showing a list of users

By selecting a user, you can choose libraries or the user's personal folders to back up, as shown in Figure 3-16. Also note the checkbox that gives you the option to make a system image, just as if you selected the *Let Windows choose (recommended)* option.

Figure 3-16 Single user, showing some of the user's libraries/folders

Once you complete the wizard, Windows starts backing up your files. While the backup runs, you can monitor its process with an exciting and handy progress bar

(Figure 3-17). If you can't handle that much excitement, you can close the backup window while the OS backs up files. The process can take a long time, even hours on a modern system with a large hard drive.

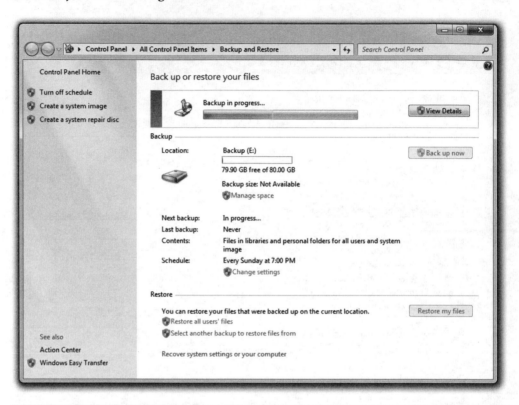

Figure 3-17 Backup in progress …

With a successful backup safe in hand, you can then use System Image Recovery to restore your system after a catastrophe. You can access it in two ways: from WinRE's menu of recovery tools or the *Restore your computer* radio button on the initial screen of the Recovery Environment, as shown in Figure 3-18.

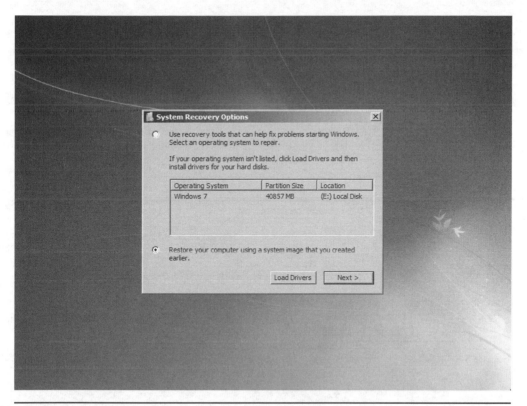

Figure 3-18 Selecting the Restore your computer using a system image... option

Both methods take you to the same wizard-based utility. If you have the drive containing the system image plugged in when you first run the wizard, it should detect your latest backup and present you with the dialog in Figure 3-19. If it doesn't list a system image or it lists the wrong one, you can select an image from another date on the same disk or even a remote network share.

After you select the image you want to restore, the utility presents you with a few more options, as shown in Figure 3-20. Most importantly, you can choose to format and repartition disks. With this option selected, the utility wipes out the existing partitions and data on all disks so the restored system will get the same partitions that the backed-up system had.

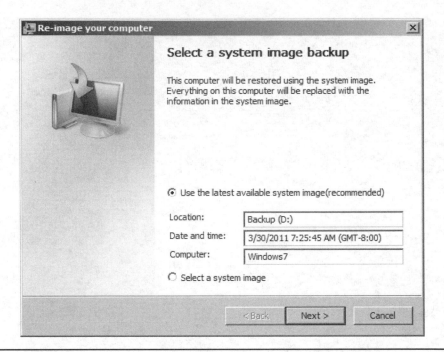

Figure 3-19   Selecting a system image

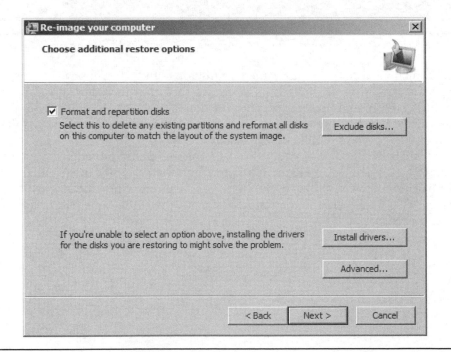

Figure 3-20   Additional restore options

After you click *Finish* on the confirmation screen (Figure 3-21), which also contains a final warning, the restore process begins (Figure 3-22). The utility removes the old system data and then copies the backed-up system image to the hard drive(s). Once the process completes, your system reboots and should start up again with all of your data and programs just where you left them when you last backed up.

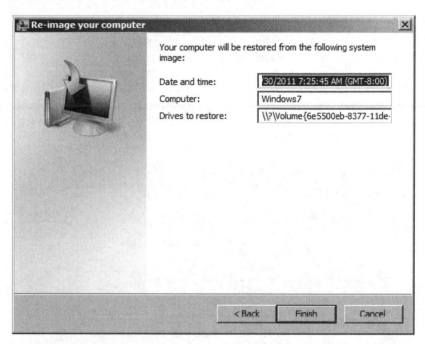

Figure 3-21   Confirming your settings

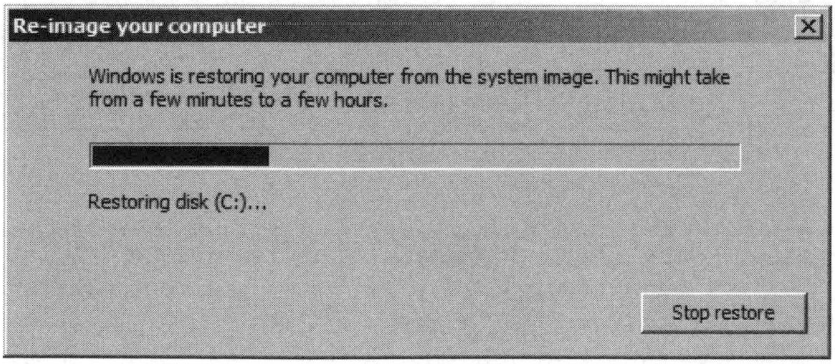

Figure 3-22   Restoring your computer

If you ever want to take advantage of the third option in the Windows Recovery Environment, make sure to run a backup that includes a system image. Remember that a system image is a complete copy of the system at the time the image was made. If you add users, applications, or other data and then restore your system from an image, anything you've done since you created that image will be lost.

Windows Memory Diagnostic

Bad RAM causes huge problems for any operating system, including Blue Screens of Death (BSoDs) and system lockups. Starting with Windows Vista, Microsoft included a memory tester to the Windows Recovery Environment. When you click the Windows Memory Diagnostic link from the main WinRE screen, it prompts you to *Restart now and check for problems (recommended)* or *Check for problems the next time I start my computer* (Figure 3-23). It doesn't really matter which option you choose, but if you think you need to test your RAM, that probably means you should do it now.

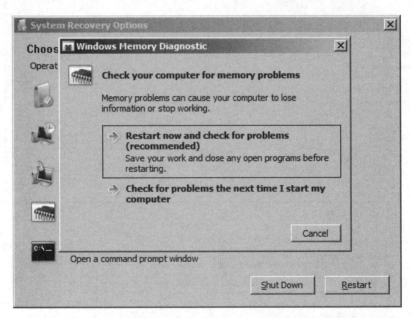

Figure 3-23 Windows Memory Diagnostic screen

Once you restart, your system immediately starts running the Windows Memory Diagnostic Tool, as shown in Figure 3-24. While the program runs, you can press F1 to see the Memory Tester options (Figure 3-25).

The tool lists three important Test Mix options at the top of the screen: Basic, Standard, and Extended. *Basic* runs quickly (about one minute) but performs only light testing. *Standard*, the default choice, takes a few minutes and tests more aggressively. *Extended* takes hours (you should let it run overnight), but it will very aggressively test your RAM.

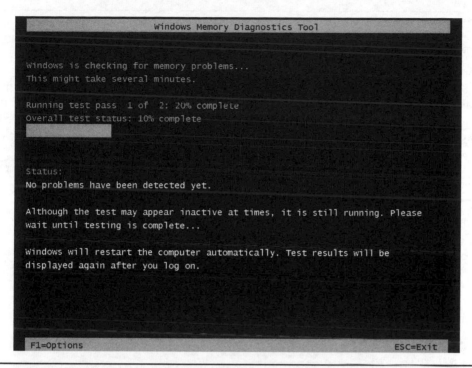

Figure 3-24 Windows Memory Diagnostic Tool running

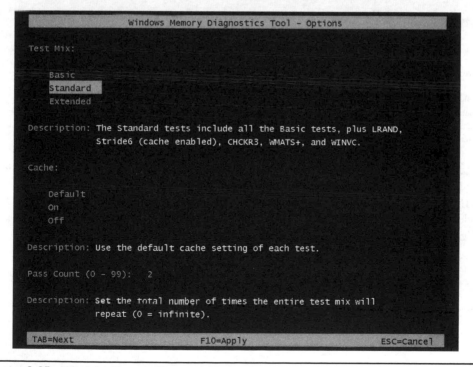

Figure 3-25 Windows Memory Diagnostic Tool options

NOTE You can also find the Windows Memory Diagnostic Tool in the Control Panel under System and Security | Administrative Tools, or start it from an administrative command prompt using the MDSCHED command.

This tool includes two other options: Cache and Pass Count. The *Cache* option enables you to set whether the tests use the CPU's built-in cache as well as override the default cache settings for each test type. Simply leave Cache set at Default and never touch it. *Pass Count* sets the number of times each set of tests will run. This option defaults to 2.

After the tool runs, your computer reboots normally. You can open Event Viewer to see the results (Figure 3-26).

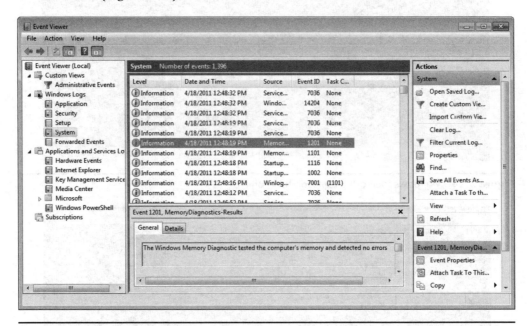

Figure 3-26 Event Viewer results

Sadly, your author has had rather poor results with the Windows Memory Diagnostic Tool. We keep lots of bad RAM around the labs here at Total Seminars, and, when put to the test, we were unable to get this tool do anything other than give us a BSoD or lock up the system. We still turn to tried-and-tested tools such as the free MEMTEST86+ when we're worried about bad RAM.

NOTE You can find out more about MEMTEST86+ at http://www.memtest.org.

Command Prompt

The last, most interesting, and easily the nerdiest option in the WinRE menu is Command Prompt. Unlike the recovery console, the WinRE command prompt is a true 32- or 64-bit prompt that functions similarly to the regular command prompt. WinRE's command prompt, however, includes an important utility (BOOTREC) that you can't find in the regular command prompt. The WinRE command prompt also lacks a large number of tools you'd have in a regular Windows command prompt (though all the important ones remain). Let's begin by looking at the BOOTREC command. After that, we'll look at some other utilities that the WinRE command prompt offers.

 NOTE The Startup Repair tool runs many of these command prompt utilities automatically. You need to use the WinRE command prompt only for unique situations where the Startup Repair tool fails.

It's important for you to understand that the CompTIA A+ exams do not expect you to know everything about all these command prompt utilities. The CompTIA A+ exams expect that you do know these things, however:

- Which utilities are available and their names
- How to access these utilities (WinRE, regular command prompt)
- What these utilities basically do
- Some of the basic switches used for these utilities
- With higher level support, that you can fix computers using these tools (being led by a specialist tech over the phone, for example)

BOOTREC BOOTREC (BOOTREC.EXE) is a Windows Recovery Environment troubleshooting and repair tool that repairs the master boot record, boot sector, or BCD store. It replaces the old FIXBOOT and FIXMBR recovery console commands and adds two more repair features.

- **BOOTREC /FIXBOOT** Rebuilds the boot sector for the active system partition.
- **BOOTREC /FIXMBR** Rebuilds the master boot record for the system partition.
- **BOOTREC /SCANOS** Looks for Windows installations not currently in the BCD store and shows you the results without doing anything.
- **BOOTREC /REBUILDMBR** Looks for Windows installations not currently in the BCD store and gives you the choice to add them to the BCD store.

TECH TIP   Boot configuration data (BCD) files contain information about operating systems installed on a computer. In Microsoft speak, that information is called a *store* or *BCD store*. This applies to Windows Vista and Windows 7 only.

BCDEDIT   With NTLDR, you could access the BOOT.INI text file to see the Windows boot order. With BOOT.INI replaced by the BCD store, you now use a new tool called BCDEDIT to see how Windows boots. Running BCDEDIT by itself (without switches) shows the boot options. The following boot information comes from a system with a single copy of Windows installed. Note there are two sections: the Windows Boot Manager section describes the location of BOOTMGR and the Windows Boot Loader section describes the location of the WINLOAD.EXE file.

EXAM TIP   Instead of editing the BOOT.INI text file, Windows 7 includes the BCDEDIT program for editing the BCD store.

```
Windows Boot Manager
--------------------
identifier              {bootmgr}
device                  partition=\Device\HarddiskVolume1
description             Windows Boot Manager
locale                  en-US
inherit                 {globalsettings}
default                 {current}
resumeobject            {d4539c9b-481a-11df-a981-a17cb98be35c}
displayorder            {current}
toolsdisplayorder       {memdiag}
timeout                 30

Windows Boot Loader
-------------------
identifier              {current}
device                  partition=C:
path                    \Windows\system32\winload.exe
description             Windows 7
locale                  en-US
inherit                 {bootloadersettings}
recoverysequence        {d4539c9d-481a-11df-a981-a17cb98be35c}
recoveryenabled         Yes
osdevice                partition=C:
systemroot              \Windows
resumeobject            {d4539c9b-481a-11df-a981-a17cb98be35c}
nx                      OptIn
```

To make changes to the BCD store, you need to use switches.

- BCDEDIT /EXPORT <filename> exports a copy of the BCD store to a file. This is a very good idea whenever you use BCDEDIT!

- BCDEDIT /IMPORT <filename> imports a copy of the BCD store back into the store.

If you look carefully at the previous BCDEDIT output, you'll notice that each section has an identifier such as {bootmgr} or {current}. You can use these identifiers to make changes to the BCD store using the /SET switch. Here's an example:

```
BCDEDIT /SET {current} path \BackupWindows\system32\winload.exe
```

This changes the path of the {current} identifier to point to an alternative WINLOAD.EXE.

BCDEDIT supports multiple OSes. Notice how this BCD store has three identifiers: {bootmgr}, {current}, and {ntldr}—a fairly common dual-boot scenario.

```
Windows Boot Manager
--------------------
identifier              {bootmgr}
device                  partition=D:
description             Windows Boot Manager
locale                  en-US
inherit                 {globalsettings}
default                 {current}
resumeobject            {60b80a52-8267-11e0-ad8a-bdb414c1bf84}
displayorder            {ntldr}
                        {current}
toolsdisplayorder       {memdiag}
timeout                 30

Windows Legacy OS Loader
------------------------
identifier              {ntldr}
device                  partition=D:
path                    \ntldr
description             Earlier Version of Windows

Windows Boot Loader
-------------------
identifier              {current}
device                  partition=C:
path                    \Windows\system32\winload.exe
description             Windows 7
locale                  en-US
inherit                 {bootloadersettings}
recoverysequence        {60b80a54-8267-11e0-ad8a-bdb414c1bf84}
recoveryenabled         Yes
osdevice                partition=C:
systemroot              \Windows
resumeobject            {60b80a52-8267-11e0-ad8a-bdb414c1bf84}
nx                      OptIn
```

A BCD store like this will cause the following menu to pop up at boot (Figure 3-27). In this case, you can use the BCDEDIT command to show the display order of the menu:

```
BCDEDIT /DISPLAYORDER [WindowsXP} /addfirst
```

You can also use BCDEDIT to set the default OS:

```
BCDEDIT /DEFAULT {current}
```

You can even remove one of the identifiers, preventing others from booting to that OS:

```
BCDEDIT /DELETE {WindowsXP}
```

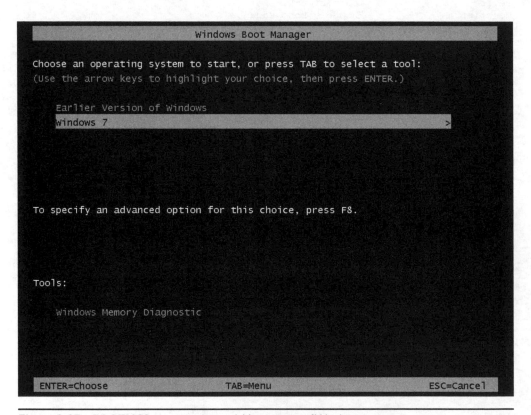

Figure 3-27   BOOTMGR showing the available versions of Windows

BCDEDIT is a tricky tool to use. To make your life easier, consider using the popular EasyBCD program from NeoSmart Technologies. You can run EasyBCD only from within a normal Windows boot, not the WinRE, but it provides more power and safety than BCDEDIT (Figure 3-28).

 NOTE   You can find EasyBCD at http://www.neosmart.net.

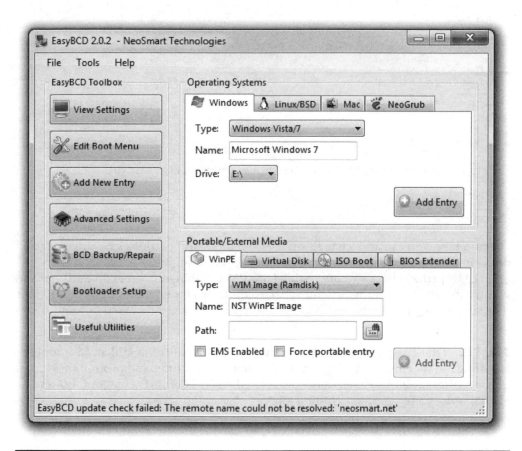

Figure 3-28   EasyBCD at work

DISKPART Command prompt also includes DISKPART, a fully featured partitioning tool. This tool lacks many of the safety features built into Disk Management, so proceed with caution. You can, for example, delete any partition of any type at any time. Starting DISKPART opens a special command prompt as shown here:

```
C:\Windows\system32>diskpart
Microsoft DiskPart version 6.1.7600
Copyright (C) 1999-2008 Microsoft Corporation.
On computer: MIKESPC
DISKPART>
```

You can list volumes (or partitions on Basic disks):

```
DISKPART> list volume
  Volume ###  Ltr  Label        Fs     Type        Size     Status     Info
  ----------  ---  -----------  -----  ----------  -------  ---------  --------
  Volume 0    D                        DVD-ROM        0 B   No Media
  Volume 1    C    New Volume   NTFS   Partition   1397 GB  Healthy    System

DISKPART>
```

Select a volume to manipulate (you may also select an entire drive):

```
DISKPART> select volume 1
Volume 1 is the selected volume.
DISKPART>
```

From here, you can add, change, or delete volumes and partitions on drives, mount or dismount volumes, and even manipulate software-level RAID arrays.

CLEAN, perhaps the most interesting DISKPART command, wipes all partition and volume information off the currently selected disk. This tool handles nasty corruptions that simply won't let Windows boot and serves as my last ditch step before I toss a drive.

FSUTIL DISKPART handles volumes and partitions, but you still need a tool for handling file systems. Both WinRE as well as the regular command prompt provide all of the typical utilities such as COPY, MOVE, DEL and FORMAT. One tool, however—FSUTIL—does a few more interesting jobs.

- FSUTIL FSINFO provides a detailed query about the drives and volumes.

- FSUTIL DIRTY <drivename> tells you if Windows considers the drive to be "dirty"—meaning you need to run AUTOCHK at the next reboot. When Windows detects an error in the file system for a drive, it flags that drive as a *dirty drive* or *dirty volume*. AUTOCHK is the disk checking utility that runs after a reboot and before Windows loads and will correct errors in the file system of a drive.

- FSUTIL REPAIR INITIATE <drive letter> runs a basic version of CHKDSK without rebooting.

ICACLS/CACLS   ICACLS in Windows Vista and Windows 7 is a command prompt tool that enables you to set NTFS permissions (Windows refers to them as access control lists, or ACLs). ICACLS is incredibly complex to use, but if, for example, you want to give user TIMMY Read, Write, and Execute privileges on a file called C:\Users\Timmy\ Desktop\TIMMY.TXT, you would type the following:

```
icacls C:\Users\Timmy\Desktop\TIMMY.TXT /grant TIMMY:(R,W,X)
```

> **NOTE**   Earlier versions of Windows used the CACLS command, rather than ICACLS.

REG   REG enables you to manipulate the registry from a command prompt. You can import, export, add, delete, and edit parts of the registry. The following example exports a part of the registry to a file called MikeStuff.REG:

```
reg export HKLM\Software\TotalSem\TTS MikeStuff.REG
```

REG doesn't do anything to the registry that REGEDIT cannot also do. REG is much better than REGEDIT, however, when you know exactly what you want to do in the registry. Just make a batch file that contains the specific REG commands you want to use and go!

HOSTNAME   What is your computer's name? Well, if you don't have a Computer menu option to right-click and select Properties to see your computer's name, finding its name is sometimes tricky. That's when the HOSTNAME utility works so nicely. Just go to a command prompt (regular or WinRE) and type HOSTNAME:

```
C:\>hostname
MikesPC
C:\>
```

Graphical Utilities in Windows RE

You might need to run a Windows program from the WinRE. Since WinRE lacks a Start button, you need to know the name of the programs you wish to run to start them at the WinRE command prompt. The two commands CompTIA wants you to know are RSTRUI and MSTSC.

RSTRUI (Figure 2-29) is the System Restore tool. It functions exactly like the System Restore option you know and love, so you don't need to run it from the WinRE prompt, but running it from a regular command prompt is handy.

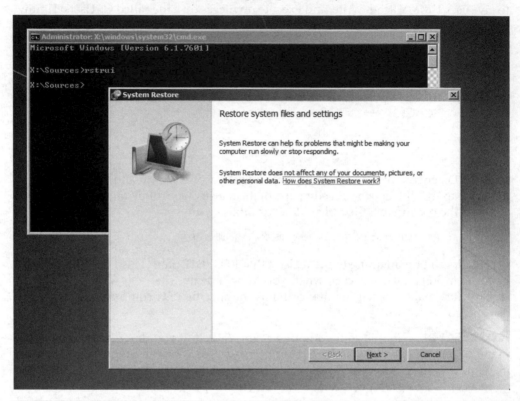

Figure 3-29 Gee, this looks familiar!

If you need to run Remote Desktop Connection from WinRE, the command is MSTSC. WinRE includes networking support, assuming WinRE has drivers for your NIC (it almost always will). With a network connection, you can use all the popular utilities like IPCONFIG, PING, and NET. But if you want to make a remote connection to another computer, you'll need to start Remote Desktop from the command prompt and use the full path as written here: **c:\windows\system32\MSTSC** (Figure 2-30).

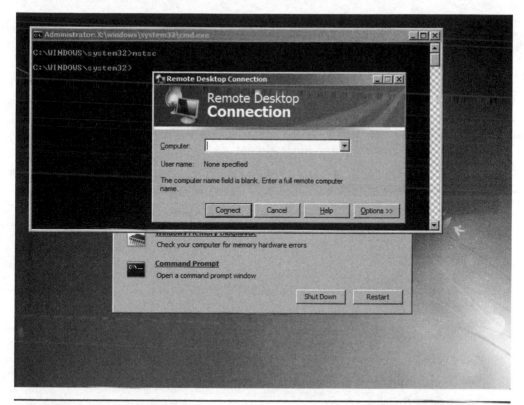

Figure 3-30   Remote Desktop

Windows RE can fix virtually any boot problem you might encounter. Microsoft did such a great job that, assuming you keep a backup and a few restore points, the chances of losing a system (short of serious hardware failure) is nearly impossible.

After Boot Problems

Other than what you learned in the original text, not much has changed with any after-boot problems you might encounter. We still use Last Known Good Configuration if possible; Safe mode is still included with Vista and 7, and naughty device drivers are easily rolled back in Device Manager. Even Event Viewer, though prettier in Windows Vista and Windows 7, still does the same job. However, Microsoft added a few new tools to the Control Panel that are extremely handy for fixing errors and issues both during and after the boot. Refer to Chapter 7 to see these tools and much more!

Chapter Review

Questions

1. Which of the following powers the Windows Recovery Environment in Windows 7?

    A. DOS

    B. Windows Preinstallation Environment

    C. System Repair

    D. BCDEdit

2. Which of the following actions does Startup Repair *not* take?

    A. Checks bad memory

    B. Runs CHKDSK

    C. Rolls back bad drivers

    D. Restores system image

3. What is the Windows 7 equivalent of Windows Vista's Windows Complete PC Restore tool?

    A. System Restore

    B. Startup Repair

    C. System Image Recovery

    D. System and Security

4. Which key do you press to open the options screen in the Windows Memory Diagnostic tool?

    A. F1

    B. F2

    C. F5

    D. F8

5. Which of the following are true about the command prompt in WinRE? (Select two.)

    A. Every command available in the normal command prompt is available in the WinRE command prompt.

    B. It supports 32-bit and 64-bit systems.

    C. It includes the BOOTREC command.

    D. It does not use switches.

6. Which of the following BOOTREC switches looks for Windows installations not in the boot store without taking other actions?

   A. /FIXBOOT

   B. /FIXMBR

   C. /SCANOS

   D. /REBUILDBCD

7. Why should you be more cautious with the DISKPART utility than with Disk Management?

   A. It automatically erases all formatting and partition information from a drive.

   B. It does not include the safety features of Disk Management.

   C. It can add and remove volumes from a drive.

   D. It can mount and dismount volumes.

8. What is the command for the command prompt's registry editor?

   A. REGEDIT

   B. REGEDIT32

   C. REG

   D. EDIT

9. Which of the following types of media is not supported by Windows 7's Backup and Restore utility?

   A. CD

   B. DVD

   C. Hard drive

   D. Tape drive

10. Which of the following choices is *not* a method of accessing the Windows Recovery Environment?

    A. System Repair disc

    B. Windows installation media

    C. Start | Control Panel | System and Security | Windows Recovery Environment

    D. Advanced Boot Options menu

Review Answers

1. **B.** WinRE is powered by the Windows Preinstallation Environment. WinRE's ancestors were powered by DOS.

2. **D.** Although Startup Repair can accomplish many things, it does not restore system images for you.

3. **C.** Windows 7's complete computer restoration tool is known as System Image Recovery.

4. **A.** Press F1 to open the options for the Windows Memory Diagnostic tool.

5. **B, C.** The command prompt in WinRE works with 32-bit and 64-bit systems. It also includes the BOOTREC command not found in normal command prompts.

6. **C.** The /SCANOS switch looks for Windows installations not in the boot store but does nothing else.

7. **B.** DISKPART is more dangerous because it does not include the safety features found in Disk Management. Deleting all the data on your hard drive is almost too easy!

8. **C.** REG is the command for the registry editor in command prompt.

9. **D.** Tape drives are not supported in the Windows 7's Backup and Restore utility.

10. **C.** You cannot access the Windows Recovery Environment from the Control Panel.

CHAPTER 4

User Account Control— From Vista to Windows 7

This chapter ties into what you learned from

- **All-In-One:** Chapter 16
- **Managing and Troubleshooting:** Chapter 16
- **Meyers' Guide to 702:** Chapter 7

W hen picking the poster child for the "327 Reasons We Hated Vista" list, I'll bet most folks put Vista's User Account Control (UAC) at the very top. Vista's UAC manifested as a pop-up dialog box that seemed to appear every time you tried to do *anything* on a Windows Vista system (Figure 4-1).

Figure 4-1
UAC in action.
Arrgh!

It's too bad that UAC got such a bad rap. Not only is UAC an important security update, but it is also a common feature in both Mac OS and Linux/Unix. Figure 4-2 shows the equivalent feature on a Mac.

Figure 4-2
UAC equivalent
on a Mac

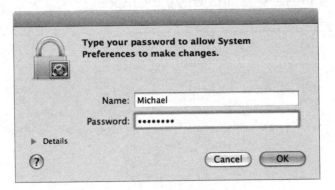

If every other major operating system uses something like UAC, why was Microsoft slammed so hard when they unveiled UAC in Windows Vista? The reason is simple: Windows users are spoiled rotten, and, until UAC came along, the vast majority of users had no idea how risky their computing behavior was.

The problem started years ago when Microsoft created the powerful NT file system (NTFS). NTFS uses robust user accounts and enables fine control over how users access files and folders—but at a cost: NTFS in its pure form is somewhat complicated. To share a folder, you need to make sure the person accessing that folder has a user account and that you've configured the NTFS permissions to give that user the permissions needed to do whatever he or she wants to do (Figure 4-3).

Figure 4-3
Typically confusing settings for NTFS permissions

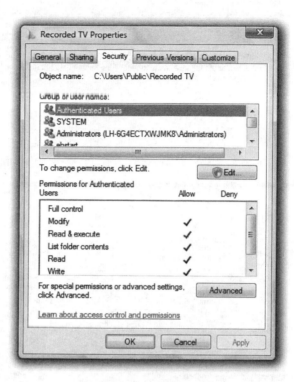

User accounts have always been a bit of a challenge. The only account that can truly do *anything* on a Windows system is the Administrator. Sure, you can configure a system with groups and assign NTFS permissions to those groups—and this is commonly done on large networks with a full-time IT staff—but what about small offices and home networks? These users almost never have the skill sets to deal with the complexities of users and groups, which often results in systems where the user accounts are all assigned Administrator privileges by default—and that's when it gets dangerous (Figure 4-4).

This chapter discusses the importance of User Account Control and examines the changes made to it for Windows 7. I'll also explain how to configure UAC to your desired security level.

Figure 4-4 The danger of Administrator privileges in the wrong hands!

UAC in Windows Vista

User Account Control enables users to know when they are about to do something that has serious consequences. The Microsoft TechNet library ("Understanding and Configuring User Account Control in Windows Vista") provides examples of common actions that require Administrator privileges:

- Installing and uninstalling applications
- Installing a driver for a device (e.g., a digital camera driver)
- Installing Windows Updates
- Configuring Parental Controls
- Installing an ActiveX control
- Adjusting Windows Firewall settings

- Changing a user's account type
- Modifying UAC settings in the Security Policy Editor snap-in (SECPOL.MSC)
- Configuring Remote Desktop access
- Adding or removing a user account
- Coping or moving files into the Program Files or Windows directory
- Scheduling Automated Tasks
- Restoring system backed-up files
- Configuring Automatic Updates
- Browsing to another user's directory

Before Vista, Microsoft invented the idea of the Power Users group to give users almost all of the power of an Administrator account (to handle most of the situations just described) without actually giving users the full power of the account. Assigning a user to the Power Users group still required someone who knew how to do this, however, so most folks at the small office/home level simply ignored the Power Users group (Figure 4-5).

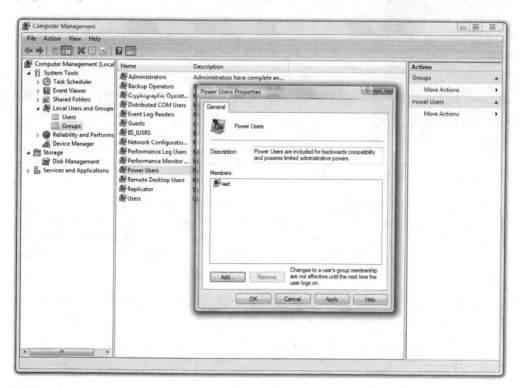

Figure 4-5 Power Users group—almost never used at the small office/home level

In Windows XP, Microsoft caved into the idea of making everyone an Administrator. Whenever you made a new account via the User Accounts Control Panel applet (Figure 4-6), you had a choice between Administrator (default) and Limited (User) accounts.

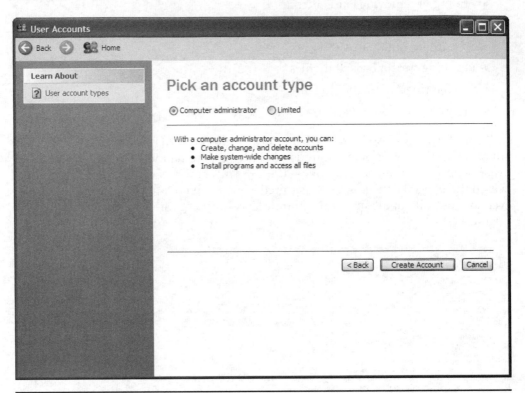

Figure 4-6 Creating a new user in XP

Clearly, Microsoft needed a better method to prevent people from running programs that they should not run. If users have the correct privileges, however—or the ability to "escalate" their privileges to that of an Administrator—then they should be able to do what they need to do as simply as possible. Microsoft needed to make the following changes:

- The idea of using an Administrator account for daily use needed to go away.
- Any level of account should be able to do anything as easily as possible.
- If a regular account wants to do something that requires Administrator privileges, the user of the regular account will need to enter the Administrator password.
- If a user with Administrator privileges wants to run something that requires Administrator privileges, the user will not have to reenter his or her password,

but the user will have to respond to an "Are you sure?"-type dialog so he or she appreciates the gravity of the action—thus, the infamous UAC dialog box.

UAC was just one part of an overall strategy to limit the number of Administrator accounts on a system. The introduction of UAC coincided with two major changes in the way new accounts were created. First, you only created an Administrator account during the Windows installation process (normally). Windows disabled the Administrator account by default. (You could also add regular users during the installation process.)

Second, all other accounts were plain, Standard user accounts by default (Figure 4-7), simplifying your choices. You could still use the old Windows NT/2000/XP groups (Power Users, Users, Guests, etc.), but you needed to dig deep into the User Accounts Control Panel applet to access them.

 NOTE All references to Control Panel applets in Windows Vista assume you are using Classic View.

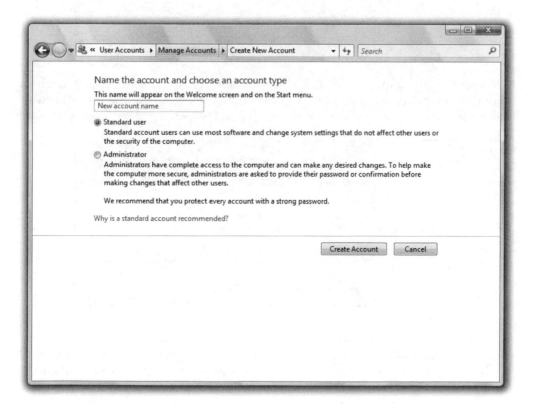

Figure 4-7 Creating a Standard user in Vista

How UAC Works

UAC works for both Standard user accounts and Administrator accounts. If a Standard user attempts to do something that requires Administrator privileges, he or she sees a UAC dialog box that prompts for the Administrator password (Figure 4-8).

Figure 4-8
Prompting for a
password in Vista

If a user with Administrator privileges attempts to do something that requires Administrator privileges, a simpler UAC dialog box appears, like the one shown in Figure 4-9.

Figure 4-9
Classic UAC
prompt

 TECH TIP The official name for the UAC dialog box is the "UAC consent prompt." When the UAC consent prompt appears in Vista, the rest of the Desktop darkens and you cannot take any other action until you respond to the consent prompt.

Interestingly, Vista has not one but four different UAC prompts, depending on the program/feature you wish to run:

UAC Classification	Type of Program
Blocked program	A program that has been blocked by a security policy
Unverified	An unknown third-party program
Verified	A digitally signed, third-party program or noncore OS program
Published by Vista	A program that is a core part of the operating system

Blocked programs generate a scary-looking, red-bannered dialog like the one shown in Figure 4-10. Note the only button you can click is Close.

Figure 4-10
Blocked program

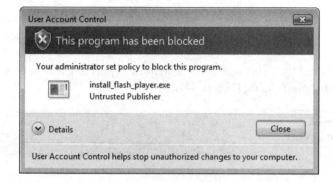

Unverified programs lack any form of certificate to validate. In this case, you get a yellow-bannered dialog box warning you the application is unsigned and giving you two options: allow the program to run (Yes) or not (No). See Figure 4-11 for an example of this.

Figure 4-11
Unverified
program

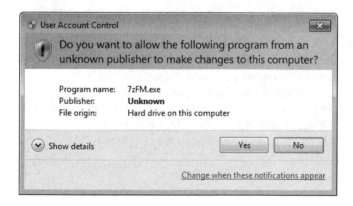

Verified programs aren't part of the core of Vista and are usually written by third-parties. These programs do have valid, verified certificates. You can identify the dialog box by its gray-blue banner (Figure 4-12).

Figure 4-12
Verified program

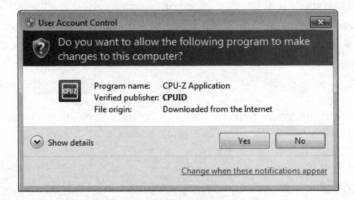

Published by Vista programs are written as part of the core of Vista and show up with a teal-bannered dialog (Figure 4-13).

Figure 4-13
Published by Vista

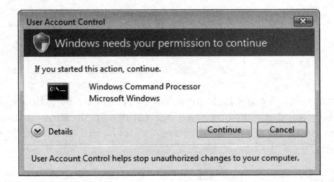

UAC uses small shield icons to warn you ahead of time that it will prompt you before certain tasks, as shown in Figure 4-14. Microsoft updated this somewhat redundant feature in Windows 7, as you'll soon see.

UAC gives users running a program an opportunity to consider their actions before they move forward. It's a good thing, but spoiled Windows users aren't accustomed to something that makes them consider their actions. As a result, one of the first things everyone learned to do when Vista came out was how to turn off UAC.

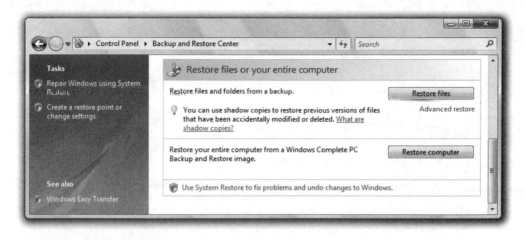

Figure 4-14   Shield icons in the Control Panel

How to Turn Off UAC

You can turn off UAC in a number of ways in Windows Vista. Here are the two most common ways:

1. In the User Accounts Control Panel applet, you'll see an option to *Turn User Account Control on or off* (Figure 4-15). Select this option and uncheck the checkbox to turn UAC off. Check the checkbox to turn it on again.

Figure 4-15   Turn User Account Control on or off

2. Open up the System Configuration utility (MSCONFIG) and select *Disable UAC*, as shown in Figure 4-16. You'll have to reboot for the changes to take effect. Note you can also turn on UAC from the System Configuration utility.

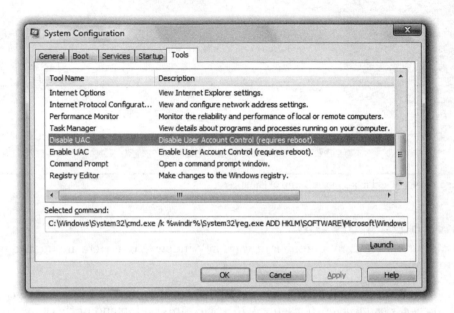

Figure 4-16 Disabling UAC in the System Configuration utility

UAC in Windows Vista worked well, but it startled users. Suddenly, users had to deal with UAC, and they didn't like that. Most users simply turned UAC off and added it to the reasons to not like Windows Vista.

UAC in Windows 7

Microsoft may be a huge company, but it still knows how to react when its customers speak out about features they don't like. Windows 7 unveiled a more refined, less "in-your-face" UAC that makes the feature much easier to use.

NOTE All references to Control Panel applets in Windows 7 assume you are using the Small Icon view.

Microsoft changed UAC with Windows 7, enabling you to adjust the consent form appearance to four different personal preference levels.

A More Granular UAC

Microsoft did some research on why UAC drove users nuts, concluding that the problem wasn't UAC itself but the "I'm constantly in your face or you can turn me off and you get no help at all" aspect. To make UAC less aggressive, Microsoft introduced four UAC levels. To see these levels, go to the User Accounts applet and select Change User Account Control settings, as shown in Figure 4-17. When you select this option, you see the dialog in Figure 4-18.

Figure 4-17   Change User Account Control settings

In Figure 4-18, you can see a slider with four levels. The top level (Always notify) means you want UAC to work exactly as it does in Vista, displaying the aggressive consent form every time you do anything that typically requires Administrator access. The bottom option (Never notify) turns off UAC. The two levels in the middle are new and are very similar. Both of them do the following:

- Do not notify me when I make changes.
- Notify me only when programs try to makes changes.

The only difference is in *how* they show the change. The second-from-top level will display the typical consent form, but only when programs try to make changes. The third-from-top level displays a consent form, but where the normal consent form dims your Desktop and doesn't allow you to do anything but address the form, this consent form just pops up like a normal dialog box.

EXAM TIP   Make sure you know what each of the four UAC levels does.

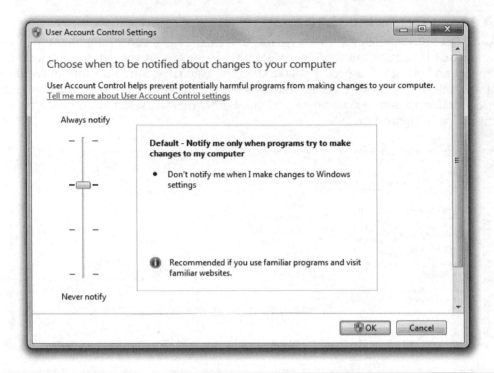

Figure 4-18 Four levels of UAC

Program Changes vs. Changes I Make

So what's the difference between a program making a change and you making a change? Take a look at Figure 4-19. In this case, Windows 7 is set to the second-from-top option. A program (the very safe and, judging by the color of the banner, verified) Adobe Download Manager is attempting to install a feature into Internet Explorer. Because this is a program trying to make changes, the UAC consent form appears and darkens the Desktop.

Figure 4-19
Darkened UAC

If you lower the UAC to the third-from-top option, you still see a consent form, but now it acts like a typical dialog (Figure 4-20).

Figure 4-20
Non-darkened
UAC

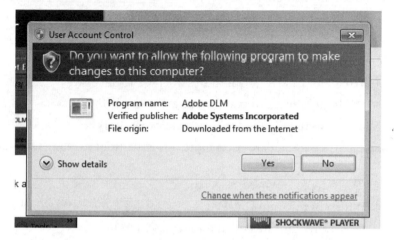

>
>
> **EXAM TIP** The default behavior for UAC in Windows 7 is the second-from-top option, which results in a screen similar to Figure 4-19.

A program such as the Adobe program described earlier is very different from a feature *you* want to change. Notice the shields, as shown earlier in Figure 4-17.

Each of these options isn't a program—each is merely a feature built into Windows. Those shields tell you that clicking the feature next to a shield will require Administrator privileges. If you were to pick the Vista-strength UAC option, you'd get a UAC consent prompt when you click one of those features. If you set UAC to any of the three lower settings, however, you'd go straight to that feature without *any* form of UAC consent prompt. Of course, this isn't true if you don't have Administrator privileges. If you're a Standard user, you'll still be prompted for a password, just as in Vista.

Overall, the improvements to UAC in Windows 7 show that it has a place on everyone's computer. UAC might cause an occasional surprise or irritation, but that one more "Are you sure?" could mean the difference between safe and unsafe computing. So go ahead, turn UAC back on in Windows 7! UAC is well worth the small inconvenience.

Chapter Review

Questions

1. Which file system uses permissions to secure files and folders?

   A. FAT16

   B. FAT32

   C. UAC

   D. NTFS

2. In Windows XP, what was the default account type?

    A. Administrator

    B. Power User

    C. Limited User

    D. Guest

3. What are some of the purposes of UAC? (Select two.)

    A. To alert users who are about to do something that has serious consequences

    B. To secure files and folders from other users

    C. To give Standard users more power without needing to make them Administrators

    D. To replace Windows Defender

4. Which of the following UAC levels are available in Windows Vista?

    A. Always on, Unverified programs only, Off

    B. On, Off

    C. Always on, Notify when I make changes, Notify when programs make changes, Off

    D. None; UAC was not implemented until Windows 7.

5. Besides Control Panel, which utility is used to turn UAC on and off?

    A. System Configuration utility (MSCONFIG)

    B. Windows IP Configuration utility (IPCONFIG)

    C. System Information utility (MSINFO32)

    D. Microsoft Security Essentials utility (MSASCUI)

6. In Windows 7, how do the two middle UAC levels differ?

    A. One creates a prompt for verified programs; the other creates a prompt for unverified programs.

    B. One uses a consent prompt that blocks all other actions; the other uses a consent prompt that does not block other actions.

    C. One creates a prompt that requires a password; the other creates a prompt that does not require a password.

    D. One uses a prompt for Standard users only; the other uses a prompt for all users.

7. Windows uses which symbol to signify an action that requires Administrator privileges?

    A. Arrow

    B. Window

    C. Compass

    D. Shield

8. Which of the following are actions that require Administrative privileges? (Select two.)

    A. Installing applications

    B. Adjusting any settings in Control Panel

    C. Scheduling Automated Tasks

    D. Downloading files from the Internet

9. What is a Blocked program?

    A. A program that has been uninstalled

    B. A program that requires an Administrator password

    C. A program that has been blocked by a security policy

    D. A program that is incompatible with Windows

10. In Windows 7, what is the only time that an Administrator account is the default option when creating new user accounts?

    A. During the Windows 7 installation

    B. When logged in as an Administrator

    C. When logged in as a Standard user

    D. When UAC is turned to the Always on setting

Review Answers

1. **D.** NTFS is a file system that uses permissions to secure files and folders.

2. **A.** In Windows XP, the default account type was Administrator.

3. **A, C.** UAC is intended to both warn users that their actions might have serious consequences and give more power to Standard users without needing to make them Administrators.

4. **B.** In Windows Vista, you can turn UAC on or off.

5. **A.** You can use MSCONFIG to turn UAC on and off.

6. **B.** One level creates a prompt that darkens the screen and blocks other actions, whereas the other uses a normal dialog that does not block any actions.

7. **D.** A shield is used to designate any actions that require Administrator privileges.

8. **A, C.** You need to be an Administrator to install applications and schedule Automated Tasks.

9. **C.** A Blocked program is a program that has been blocked by a security policy.

10. **A.** The only time that the default account type is an Administrator account is during installation.

CHAPTER 5

IPv6

This chapter ties into what you learned from

- **All-in-One:** Chapter 23
- **Managing and Troubleshooting:** Chapter 23
- **Meyers' Guide to 701:** Chapter 16
- **Meyers' Guide to 702:** Chapter 13

When the early developers of the Internet set out to create an addressing or naming scheme for devices on the Internet, they faced several issues. Of course they needed to determine how the numbers or names worked, and for that they developed the Internet Protocol (IP) and IP addresses. But beyond that, They had to determine how many computers might exist in the future, and then make the IP address space even bigger to give the Internet naming serious longevity. But how many computers would exist in the future?

Keep in mind that TCP/IP development took place back in the early 1970s. There were fewer than 1000 computers in the entire *world* at the time, but that didn't keep the IP developers from thinking big! They decided to go absolutely crazy (as many people considered it at the time) and, in 1979, created the *Internet Protocol version 4* (*IPv4*) 32-bit IP address space, creating approximately 4 billion IP addresses. That should have been fine for the foreseeable future!

It wasn't. First, the TCP/IP folks wasted huge chunks of IP addresses due to classful addressing and an easygoing, wasteful method of parceling out IP addresses. Second, the Internet reached a level of popularity far beyond the original developers' imaginations. By the mid-1980s, the rate of consumption for IP addresses started to worry the Internet people and the writing was on the wall for IPv4's 32-bit addressing.

As a result, the Internet Engineering Task Force (IETF) developed a new IP addressing scheme called *Internet Protocol version 6* (*IPv6*) that is slowly replacing IPv4. IPv6 extends the 32-bit IP address space to 128 bits, allowing up to 2^{128} (that's close to 3.4×10^{38}) addresses! That should hold us for the foreseeable future! This number—3.4×10^{38} addresses—is something like all the grains of sand on Earth or 1/8 of all the molecules in the atmosphere.

NOTE If you really want to know how many IP addresses IPv6 provides, here's your number: 340,282,366,920,938,463,463,374,607,431,768,211,456.

Although they achieve the same function—enabling computers on IP networks to send packets to each other—IPv6 and IPv4 differ a lot when it comes to implementation. This chapter begins by dissecting IPv6 address notation, and then looks at the ways a computing device can obtain valid IPv6 addresses. The chapter finishes by examining how routers running IPv6 can use a feature called aggregation to dramatically speed up the Internet for everyone.

IPv6 Address Notation

The 32-bit IPv4 addresses are written as 197.169.94.82, using four octets. The 128-bit IPv6 addresses are written like this:

```
2001:0000:0000:3210:0800:200C:00CF:1234
```

IPv6 uses a colon as a separator, instead of the period used in IPv4's dotted-decimal format. Each "group" is a hexadecimal number between 0000 and FFFF called, unofficially, a *hextet*.

NOTE For those who don't play with hex regularly, one hexadecimal character (for example, *F*) represents 4 bits, so four hexadecimal characters make a 16-bit group. For some reason, the IPv6 developers didn't provide a name for the "group of four hexadecimal characters," so many techs and writers have taken to calling them "hextets" to distinguish them from IPv4 "octets."

A complete IPv6 address always has eight hextets of four hexadecimal characters. If this sounds like you're going to type in really long IP addresses, don't worry. IPv6 offers a number of ways to shorten the address in written form.

 EXAM TIP IPv4 addresses use 32 bits, and IPv6 addresses use 128 bits. Be sure you can identify their address length differences and address conventions.

First, leading zeroes can be dropped from any hextet, so 00CF becomes CF and 0000 becomes 0. Let's rewrite the previous IPv6 address using this shortening method:

`2001:0:0:3210:800:200C:CF:1234`

Second, you can remove one or more consecutive hextets of all zeroes, leaving the two colons together. For example, using the :: rule, you can write the IPv6 address:

`2001:0:0:3210:800:200C:CF:1234`

as

`2001::3210:800:200C:CF:1234`

You can remove any number of consecutive hextets of zeroes to leave a double colon, but you can only use this trick *once* in an IPv6 address.

Take a look at this IPv6 address:

`FEDC:0000:0000:0000:00CF:0000:BA98:1234`

Using the double-colon rule, I have four hextets of zeroes that can I can reduce; three of them follow the FEDC and the fourth comes after 00CF. Because of the "only use once" stipulation, my best and shortest option is to convert the address to:

`FEDC::CF:0:BA98:1234`

I may not use a second :: to represent the fourth hextet of zeroes—only one :: is allowed per address! This rule exists for a good reason. If more than one :: was used, how could you tell how many hextets of zeroes were in each group? Answer: you couldn't.

Here's an example of a very special IPv6 address that takes full advantage of the double-colon rule, the IPv6 loopback address:

`::1`

Without using the double-colon nomenclature, this IPv6 address would look like this:

`0000:0000:0000:0000:0000:0000:0000:0001`

NOTE The unspecified address (all zeroes) can never be used, and neither can an address that contains all ones (in binary) or all *F*s (in IPv6 notation).

IPv6 still uses subnets, but you won't find a place to type in 255s anywhere. IPv6 uses the "/*x*" Classless Inter-Domain Routing (CIDR) nomenclature where the /*x* refers to the number of bits in the subnet mask, just like in IPv4. Here's how to write an IP address and subnet for a typical IPv6 host:

```
FEDC::CF:0:BA98:1234/64
```

Where Do IPv6 Addresses Come From?

With IPv4, IP addresses come from one of two places: either you type in the IP address yourself (*static IP addressing*) or you use the Dynamic Host Configuration Protocol (DHCP, also called *dynamic IP addressing*). With IPv6, addressing works very differently. Instead of one IP address, you can have up to three IP addresses on a single network card, although two is by far the most common.

When a computer running IPv6 first boots up, it gives itself a *link-local address*, IPv6's equivalent to IPv4's Automatic Private IP Addressing (APIPA) address. Although an APIPA address can indicate a loss of network connectivity or a problem with the DHCP server, computers running IPv6 always have a link-local address. The first 64-bits of a link-local address are always FE80::. That means every address always begins with FE80:0000:0000:0000. If your operating system supports IPv6 and IPv6 is enabled, you can see this address. Figure 5-1 shows the link-local address for a typical system running the IPCONFIG utility.

Figure 5-1 Link-local address in IPCONFIG

TECH TIP Every computer running IPv6 will always have at least a link-local address.

The folks who designed IPv6 gave operating system makers a choice on how to make the last 64-bits of an IPv6 address. The first method uses a random value—and this is the way Windows does it. When you install Windows, it simply makes a random value for the last 64-bits of the IPv6 address. Once created, this unique 64-bit value will never change.

The alternative method to create the IPv6 address uses the MAC address of the network card. Be warned! The CompTIA A+ exams are Windows-centric, and Windows does not use this second method by default. Even though Windows does not currently use this method by default, understanding this is critical to understanding IPv6.

NOTE If you want to force Windows to use the MAC address, just go to a command prompt and type this:

```
netsh interface ipv6 set global randomizeidentifiers=disabled
```

Using the MAC addresses to create the last 64-bits of an IP address (called the *Extended Unique Identifier, 64-bit* or *EUI-64*) causes a little problem. The MAC address only contains 48 bits. So how does your system create the EUI-64?

1. Let's assume the MAC address is 00-0C-29-53-45-CA. Remove the dashes from the MAC address and split it in half:

   000C29   5345CA

2. Add "FFFE" in the middle:

   000C29**FFFE**5345CA

3. The third step requires a little binary knowledge. Also, take note of when I use "hexadecimal" versus "binary" in the description to follow. You convert the second hexadecimal digit, in this example, the second 0 from the left, into binary: 0 in hex = 0000 in binary. You take the third binary digit in that 0000 that you just converted and complement it, which means that if it's a 0, as in this example, you make it a 1, and if it's a 1, you make it a 0. Then convert it back to hexadecimal: 0010 = 2 in hexadecimal.

4. Put that value back in the second position:

   020C29FFFE5345CA

5. Break it into standard IPv6 format:

   020C:29FF:FE53:45CA

6. Add it to the first 64 bits and, in this example, drop the leading zeroes:

   FE80::20C:29FF:FE53:45CA

The link-local address handles all the local connections in an IPv6 network. As long as you don't need an Internet connection, the link-local address is all you need. The old concepts of static and DHCP addressing don't really make much sense in IPv6 unless you have dedicated servers (even in IPv6, servers usually still have static IP addresses). Link-local addressing takes care of all your local network needs!

IPv6 Subnet Masks

IPv6 subnets function the same as IPv4 subnets, but you need to know two new rules:

- The last 64 bits of an IPv6 address are generated randomly or using the MAC address, leaving a maximum of 64 bits for the subnet. Therefore, no subnet is ever longer than /64.

- The IANA passes out /32 subnets to big ISPs and end users who need large allotments. ISPs and others may pass out /48 and /64 subnets to end users.

Therefore, the vast majority of IPv6 subnets are between /48 and /64.

Subnet masks are just as important in IPv6 networks as they were in IPv4 networks. Unlike with IPv4 networks, however, all IPv6 networks with computers have a /64 subnet mask, so you'll rarely, if ever, need to make any changes manually.

Global Addresses

To get on the Internet, your system needs a second IPv6 address called a *global address*. The only way to get a global address is from your default gateway router, which must be configured to pass out global IPv6 addresses. When your computer boots up, it sends out a very special packet called a *router solicitation message*, looking for a router. Your router hears this message and tells your computer your network ID and subnet (together called the *prefix*). See Figure 5-2.

Figure 5-2
Getting a global address

NOTE A router solicitation message uses the address FF02::2. This address is read only by other computers running IPv6 in the network. This type of address is different from a broadcast address and is called a *multicast address*.

Once you have your prefix, your computer generates the rest of the global address to get the last 64-bits of the link-local address. You now have a legitimate, public IP address as well as a link-local address. Figure 5-3 shows the IPv6 information in Windows 7.

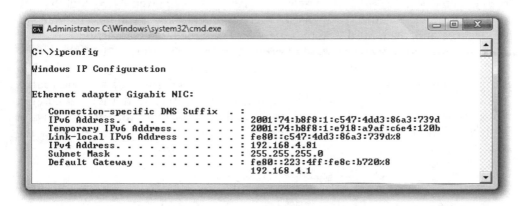

Figure 5-3 IPv6 configuration

Let's look at this process in detail with an example:

1. An IPv6-capable computer boots up. As it boots, it sends out a router solicitation message (FF02::2).

2. An IPv6-configured router hears the request and then sends the prefix to the computer. In this example, let's say it is 2001:470:b8f9:1/64.

3. The computer takes the prefix and adds the EUI-64 or a random value to the end of the prefix. If the MAC address is 00-0C-29-53-45-CA, then the address is 20C:29FF:FE53:45CA.

4. Putting the prefix with the last half of the address, you get the global address: 20 01:470:b8f9:1:20C:29FF:FE53:45CA.

 NOTE At the moment, IANA only passes out global addresses that begin with the number 2 (for example, 2001::, 2002::, and so on). As demand increases, this will certainly change, but for now, knowing a global address when you see one is easy.

A global address is a true Internet address. If another computer is running IPv6 and also has a global address, it can access your system unless you have some form of firewall.

EXAM TIP Computers using IPv6 need a global address to access the Internet.

Aggregation

Outstanding! Now that you have a basic grasp of IPv6 addresses and IPv6 subnet masks, you can understand a unique feature of IPv6 called *aggregation*. Aggregation can reduce total Internet traffic to a fraction of its current size, making IPv6 a powerful new tool that will speed up the entire Internet. To appreciate aggregation and how it will help the Internet, let's begin by understanding the problem right now with the Internet under IPv4.

Routers need to know where to send every packet they encounter. Most routers have a default path or *route* on which they send packets that aren't specifically defined to go on any other network. As you get to the top of the Internet, the tier-one routers (the monstrous routers that control the vast majority of Internet traffic) that connect to the other tier-one routers can't have any default route because they are the kings of the Internet; no other router can tell them what to do (Figure 5-4). We call these the *no-default routers.*

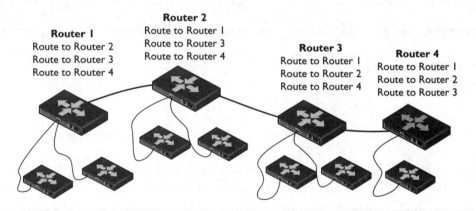

Figure 5-4 No-default routers

The current state of tier-one routers is rather messy. A typical IPv4 no-default router has somewhere around 30,000 to 50,000 entries in its *routing table* (the list of networks a router knows how to access), requiring a router with massive firepower. But what would happen if the Internet was organized as shown in Figure 5-5? Note how every router underneath a no-default router always uses a piece of that router's existing address. In other words, each router takes on a part of its address from the router above it. This is what makes aggregation so great.

Aggregation drastically reduces the size and complexity of routing tables, making the Internet faster. Using an IPv4 network, every organizations' network has dozens of interconnections. With IPv6, each organization only needs a single entry point which every network device beneath it attaches to like a tree.

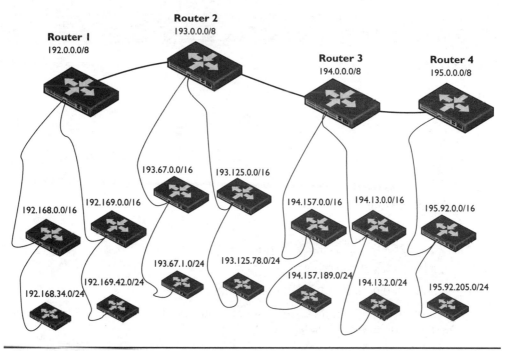

Figure 5-5 Aggregation

Imagine travelling from New York to Los Angeles. An IPv4 highway system would involve many possible routes to travel there (since multiple highways lead into Los Angeles). You wouldn't need to know every possible route, but a computer network would. With IPv6, there is only one connection between Los Angeles and New York. Since everyone knows there is only one road between these two cities, you don't need to ask for directions. Aggregation works in a similar way: the network only needs to know one route, enabling it to work much more efficiently.

IPv6 even enables the entire network to change IP addresses on-the-fly to keep everything working. If a higher-level router's IP address changes, all the routers beneath it receive a message telling them to change the relevant part of their address too. If, for example, a higher-level router's first octet (the first four numbers) changes from 2001 to 2002, the rest of the routers beneath it will change theirs too.

Thankfully, this all happens behind the scenes. Know that your IPv6 Internet addresses may suddenly change from time to time and that the address changes are a fairly rare but normal aspect of using IPv6.

IPv6 improves upon IPv4 in many ways, not the least of which is there are enough addresses for everyone (though they said that last time, too). Both protocols accomplish the same task, but go about it in very different ways using different technology and terminology. IPv6 is coming, and, as a tech, you need to be ready for it.

Chapter Review

Questions

1. How many bits comprise an IPv6 address?

    A. 32

    B. 48

    C. 64

    D. 128

2. Which of the following is a valid IPv6 address?

    A. 192.168.0.1

    B. 2001:376:BDS:0:3378:BAAF:QR9:223

    C. 2541:FDC::ACDF:2770:23

    D. 0000:0000:0000:0000:0000:0000:0000:0000

3. Which of the following IPv6 addresses are equivalent to ACCB:0876:0000:0000: FD87:0000:0000:0064? (Select two.)

    A. ACCB:876::FD87:0:0:64

    B. ACCB:876::FD87::64

    C. ACCB:876:0:0:FD87::64

    D. ACCB:876:0:FD87:0:64

4. What is the only type of IPv6 address required to communicate with other computers on a local network?

    A. Link-local

    B. Global unicast

    C. EUI-64

    D. Multicast

5. Which of the following is a valid link-local address?

    A. 2001:2323:CCE:34FF:19:DE3:2DBA:52

    B. FE80::1994:33DD:22CE:769B

    C. FEFE:0:0:0:FEFE:0:0:0

    D. FFFF:FFFF:FFFF:FFFF:232D:0:DE44:CB2

6. What is true of link-local addresses?

    A. They are passed out by the default gateway router.

    B. They are completely randomly generated by each computer.

    C. The last 64 bits are always generated from the MAC address, except on Windows Vista and Windows 7.

    D. They always start with 169.254.

7. What is a valid IPv6 subnet mask?

    A. /64

    B. /72

    C. /255

    D. 255.255.255.0

8. Which of the following IPv6 addresses are not allowed? (Select two.)

    A. 0000:0000:0000:0000:0000:0000:0000:0000

    B. FFFF:FFFF:FFFF:FFFF:FFFF:FFFF:FFFF:FFFF

    C. 2001::FA00

    D. FEEE:EEEE::3FA4:21:21

9. How many routes does a typical IPv4 no-default router's routing table have?

    A. 100

    B. 1,000

    C. 30,000

    D. 500,000

10. What effect does aggregation have on the Internet?

    A. Aggregation enhances the routing tables of no-default routers, adding entries for every other router on the Internet, thus making the Internet more robust.

    B. Aggregation simplifies the routing tables of all the routers on the Internet, thus making the Internet faster.

    C. Aggregation adds IPv6 routes to the no-default routers, enabling traffic on the Internet to use either IPv4 or IPv6.

    D. Aggregation refers to an intense amount of traffic on the Internet. It has no effect on the Internet, although it reflects the irritation of the users.

Answers

1. **D.** IPv6 addresses contain 128 bits, written in hexadecimal notation.

2. **C.** 192.168.0.1 is an IPv4 address. 2001:376:BDS:0:3378:BAAF:QR9:223 is not valid because it contains nonhexadecimal characters (S, Q, and R). An IPv6 address may not consist of all zeroes. Only 2541:FDC::ACDF:2770:23, which uses shorthand, is valid.

3. **A, C.** Both A and C properly use the double-colon shorthand to indicate consecutive groups of zeroes. B improperly uses this shorthand by using it twice. D illegally combines consecutive groups of zeroes.

4. **A.** Only a link-local address is required for non-Internet communication.

5. **B.** Link-local addresses always start with FE80::.

6. **C.** The last 64 bits of a link-local address are generated based on the MAC address, except on Windows Vista/7, where they are randomly generated.

7. **A.** No subnet is ever longer than /64, and 255.255.255.0 is an IPv4 mask.

8. **A, B.** An IPv6 address cannot consist of all zeros or all Fs.

9. **C.** A no-default router has anywhere from 30,000 to 50,000 routers in its routing table.

10. **B.** Aggregation simplifies the routing tables of all the routers on the Internet, thus making the Internet faster.

CHAPTER 6

Windows 7 Networking

This chapter ties into what you learned from

Every version of Windows covered on the CompTIA A+ exams, from Windows 2000 Professional to Windows 7 Ultimate, comes packed with powerful network functions. These network functions, based on the idea of sharing NTFS folders, enable you to control how your system shares its resources. But unless you work on a professionally administered network, all of this power—including all the necessary setup, installation, configuration, and troubleshooting—goes unused.

Microsoft has known about this issue for a long time, but only with the release of Windows 7 have we seen what Microsoft's been doing to make networking easier for those without a nerd in their pocket. To understand the power and beauty of Windows 7 networking, you need to appreciate where it came from.

In this chapter, I'm going to take you on a tour of networking through the ages of Windows, from Windows 2000 to Windows 7. Along the way, I'll explain how each version handled file sharing over a network.

Windows 2000 used NTFS permissions to share files, while Windows XP introduced Simple File Sharing. Windows Vista expanded upon this with File Sharing Wizard, and Windows 7 wrapped it all up with a neat little bow called HomeGroup. Microsoft also developed several new technologies to make all of this possible, but before I get ahead of myself, let's start with classic file sharing in Windows 2000.

Classic Folder Sharing

Let's consider the steps necessary to share a folder on a network, using the traditional process that includes NTFS folders, user accounts, and groups. In this example, we'll use Windows 2000 Professional, but every version of Windows works the same. To keep things a tad simpler, let's assume you're in a workgroup, not a member of a Windows domain. Granted, you can do this several different ways, but I like this way the most.

1. Right-click on a folder and select Properties (Figure 6-1).

Figure 6-1
Selecting
Properties

2. Click the Sharing tab. Enable sharing by selecting *Share this folder* and give the folder a share name (Figure 6-2).

Figure 6-2

Sharing tab

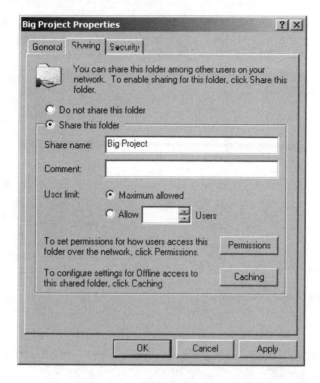

3. Click the Security tab and give NTFS permissions to whomever you want to access the folder. Assuming the person you want to share files with uses a different computer, you can either create an account using the same user name (and even the same password) on your system or create a new account for that person and tell him or her the password (Figure 6-3).

4. Using the system with which you wish to access the shared folder, click the Network Neighborhood icon to access the share (Figure 6-4).

If you have a good understanding of NTFS, workgroups, local user accounts, and networking in general, you can accomplish this easily. But if you're a *normal* person, you might have trouble. This difficulty created a tremendous amount of anxiety among home and small office users (Figure 6-5).

Since the release of Windows 2000, Microsoft has developed wizards and other tools that make data sharing easier. In Windows XP, Microsoft introduced Simple File Sharing.

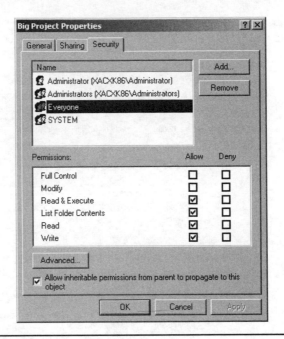

Figure 6-3 NTFS permissions

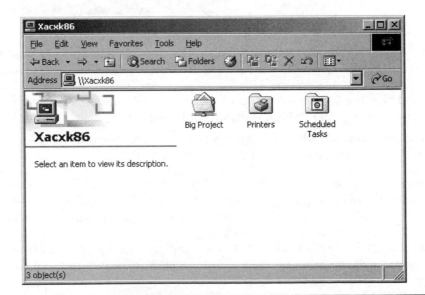

Figure 6-4 Accessing the shared folder

Figure 6-5 Josie is not at all happy.

Simple File Sharing

Windows XP's Simple File Sharing hid the intricacy of NTFS but still required you to give the folder a share name and define whether the user could make any changes to the folder. Windows XP turns Simple File Sharing on by default while in a workgroup. To use this feature, right-click on a folder and select the Sharing menu option to see a dialog box like the one shown in Figure 6-6.

Click the *Share this folder on the network* checkbox, give the folder a share name, and, if you want other people to be able to change files, click the handy *Allow network users to change my files*. That's it!

Simple File Sharing worked well, but actually harkened back to an old Microsoft network sharing method called LAN Manager. LAN Manager comes from the days of DOS and FAT file systems, clearly predating NTFS, but using it made sharing a little easier than the standard method. Figure 6-7 shows what happens to that same folder's dialog box (as shown in Figure 6-6) when you turn off Simple File Sharing in Windows XP.

 NOTE Simple File Sharing is turned on by default in Windows XP.

Unfortunately, Simple File Sharing remained too simple. It didn't employ user accounts at all—you could choose everyone or no one when it came to shares—and it ignored the finer controls of NTFS, allowing anyone with access to change anything or read anything. Microsoft created an improved file-sharing method in Windows Vista.

Figure 6-6
Simple File Sharing
in Windows XP

Figure 6-7
Simple File
Sharing turned off

File Sharing Wizard—Vista Style

Windows Vista replaced Simple File Sharing with the File Sharing Wizard. When you right-clicked on a folder in Vista and selected the Share option, you got a dialog box similar to the one shown in Figure 6-8.

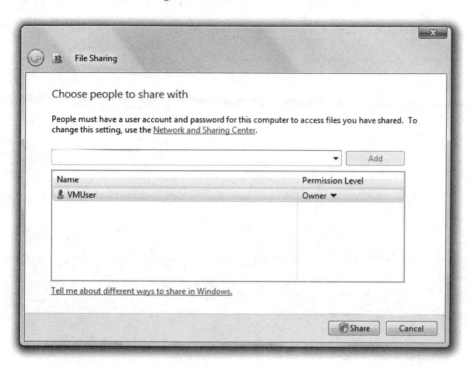

Figure 6-8   File Sharing Wizard in Vista

Vista's File Sharing Wizard reworked the idea of easy file sharing. Microsoft dumped the ancient LAN Manager tools and instead supported the real power of Windows networking. Still, Vista hid much of that power under a very clever wizard utility.

Because Vista's File Sharing Wizard used the full power of Windows networking, users couldn't ignore user accounts or NTFS permissions. In the true spirit of "Why We Should Use Wizards on Computers," Microsoft integrated two very handy features into Vista's File Sharing Wizard.

First, you had to assign one or more user accounts to share a folder. To make this easier, the wizard enabled you either to include Everyone or to Create a new user from inside the wizard—very convenient (Figure 6-9).

Second, Microsoft needed to do something about NTFS permissions to make them easy to understand and more powerful than their (lack of) implementation in Windows XP.

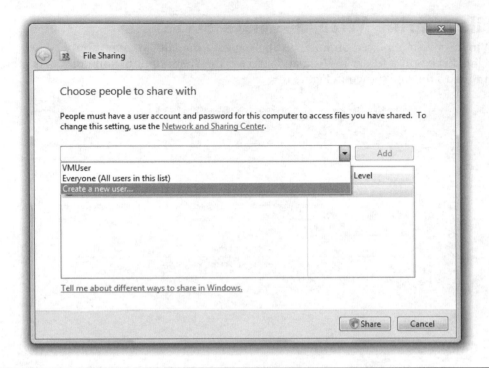

Figure 6-9   Selecting a user (or creating a new one) in Vista's File Sharing Wizard

As a compromise, Vista's File Sharing Wizard reduced NTFS permissions to four Permission Levels:

- **Owner**   Can do anything to the shared folder or anything in the shared folder
- **Reader**   Can view shared files but not change them or delete them
- **Contributor**   Can view or add files to the shared folder but can only alter or delete files he or she has contributed
- **Co-owner**   Can view, add, alter, or delete any shared file

Figure 6-10 shows Vista's File Sharing Wizard with the Permission Level being set for a second user. Notice that you can also "unshare" folders by using the Remove option in the File Sharing Wizard.

You need to understand that these Permission Levels simply cover up preconfigured NTFS settings. The wizard hides this process to make it easier for the user.

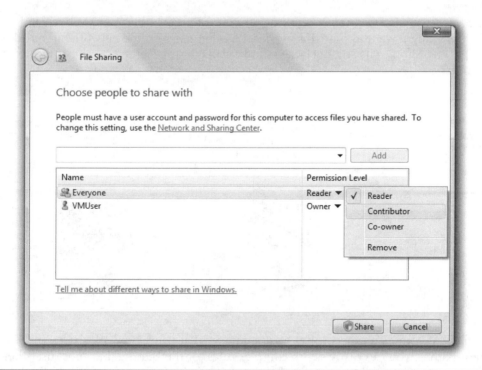

Figure 6-10 Vista Permission Levels

 NOTE The default Permission Level for the File Sharing Wizard is Reader (in both Windows Vista and Windows 7).

You need to know about this subtle difference: If Windows XP's Simple File Sharing was on, you couldn't access NTFS permissions on that folder. In Windows Vista, you could always access the NTFS permissions, whether you enabled File Sharing Wizard or not.

What Are We Sharing?

Even with tools like Simple File Sharing and the File Sharing Wizard, many users had problems with the idea of folder sharing in Windows. Most home users only want to share photos, music, videos, and the occasional document. The idea of sharing a *folder* and then putting stuff into the shared folder perhaps doesn't make sense to most folks. People want to share music, in other words, not a folder that stores music.

Most users also want to control the amount of access other people have. Bob, for example, might want to share his music with other users on the network but not share his photos. Simple File Sharing lacked this level of control. Figure 6-11 shows this typical quandary.

Figure 6-11

Bob has a problem.

Now, if you're an expert (or at least competent) at using network shares and NTFS permissions, you can easily set up complex rules for file sharing, but most users never exercised that power. Microsoft needed to come up with a simpler sharing method than pure NTFS, both more powerful than XP's Simple File Sharing, and less folder-centric than Vista's File Sharing Wizard.

 NOTE Be careful here! Windows XP, Vista, and 7 all have Simple File Sharing or the File Sharing Wizard, but Microsoft never looked at these as "The Way" to share data. Even while Microsoft improved Simple File Sharing, they put outrageous amounts of effort into technology that would make Simple File Sharing and the File Sharing Wizard obsolete. In your author's opinion, Microsoft didn't attain this goal, but they achieved a leap in network technology from Windows XP to Windows 7, which makes sharing data much easier.

Windows Rallies to the Solution

During the heyday of Windows XP, almost everyone got an Internet connection, which involved cable or DSL modems, routers, switches, and wireless devices (often the final three components would be combined into a single device), making network setup a potentially difficult process (Figure 6-12).

In response, Microsoft developed a series of tools that enabled Windows computers to "discover" what was on a network. A Windows machine that could somehow "talk" to the computers, routers, wireless access points, and other devices on your network achieved two goals. First, the process of setting up and troubleshooting networks would be much easier. Second, a Windows PC would be able to query every available device on a network (Figure 6-13).

Figure 6-12
Typical home
network setup

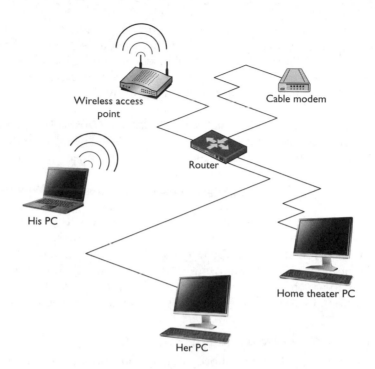

Figure 6-13
We need to talk!

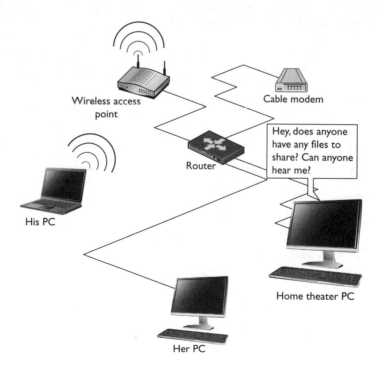

To make all of this happen, Microsoft needed to add a lot of network plumbing to Windows. In particular, Windows Vista adopted a well-known technology: *Universal Plug and Play (UPnP)*. UPnP is a tool that automates the installation and configuration of network devices (like routers, switches, and wireless access points). Microsoft didn't invent UPnP, but Vista used it more aggressively than past OSes. Along with UPnP, Microsoft also added a few of its own protocols such as *Link Layer Topology Discovery (LLTD)* and *Quality Windows Audio/Visual Experience (qWave)*. LLTD uses MAC addresses to find other devices on the network, whereas qWave determines the Quality of Service (QoS) for streaming media. Together, Microsoft named these technologies *Windows Rally*.

The Windows Rally technologies served (and still serve, in Windows 7) as the underpinnings and plumbing of Windows networking, disappearing from users (but not us techs). Rally, however, doesn't work by itself. Microsoft needed to add a number of tools to help users decide what to share. First, users needed some predetermined shared folders. Second, all of this discovery could open up users to risks on the wrong networks. Something needed to control discovery based on how much a user trusted the network to which he or she was connected. Finally, and most importantly, applications needed to help users put files in the right places so users could share them.

Public and Default Folders

You can easily predefine what people share—just use the public folders! Public folders first appeared in Windows XP, but Vista first started using the C:\USERS\PUBLIC folder with its many separate subfolders. Windows 7 uses the same C:\USERS\PUBLIC folder structure as Windows Vista (Figure 6-14).

Figure 6-14 Content of typical Windows C:\USERS\PUBLIC folder

Every user in Windows Vista/7 also has his or her own personal folders for music, video, documents, and so on (Figure 6-15).

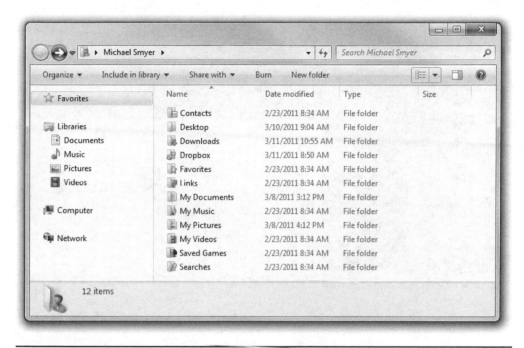

Figure 6-15 Content of a typical Windows user's personal folder

Microsoft tells programmers who make applications that use pictures, music, video, and so on, to point users to the correct default folders. That doesn't mean you can't save files anywhere you want, but rather that programs will always point to these folders by default—which most people will use. Figure 6-16, for example, shows the save feature of a photo-retouching program automatically pointing to the My Pictures folder when a user tries to save.

So now we have default folders where most people should place their photos, videos, documents, and music. For the next step, we need to deal with how the devices on the network can see what's out there via discovery because, as you're about to see, discovery can be very dangerous!

Windows Network Location

Unfortunately, Rally's network discovery technology opens you up to some new dangers. If you trust the other computers around you, discoverability enables you to share files with others safely, but in a coffee house surrounded by strange computers, you might accidentally start sharing important documents with everyone in the room (Figure 6-17).

Figure 6-16   Saving a picture to My Pictures

Microsoft needed to develop a way for you to separate trustworthy networks (like the one in your house or at the office) from nontrustworthy networks (like a public Wi-Fi Internet connection at the airport). To do this, Microsoft came up with three types of networks: Domain, Private, and Public.

1. A *Domain* network is a Windows network controlled by a Windows domain controller. In this case, the domain controller itself tells your machine what it can and cannot share. You don't need to do anything when your computer joins a domain.

2. A *Private* network enables you to share resources, discover other devices, and allow other devices to discover your computer safely.

3. A *Public* network prevents your computer from sharing and disables all discovery protocols.

Configuring Network Location

When your computer connects to a network the first time, Windows Vista and 7 will prompt you to choose what type of network: Home, Work, or Public location (Figure 6-18).

Figure 6-17
You want to
share with
these guys?

First, notice that Domain is not an option. There's a good reason for this: If your computer is on a domain, you won't see the dialog box in Figure 6-18. When your computer joins a domain, Windows automatically sets your network location to Domain (unless your domain controller choses something different, which is unlikely).

Assuming your computer connects to a workgroup and not a domain, what do you choose? Home and Work are the same (by default)—these are private networks. Microsoft possibly felt that using the terms "Work" and "Home" made more sense than "Private."

You can easily change these settings. Windows Vista and 7 differ a little here though. I'll walk you through the process in Vista here and then return to the much simpler methods in Windows 7.

Open the Network and Sharing Center from the Control Panel (Figure 6-19) and select Customize in Windows Vista. This opens the Set Network Location dialog box as shown in Figure 6-20. Notice that this dialog box simply offers the options "Public" and "Private." I imagine Microsoft assumed that if you knew enough to get this far, you also knew the difference between public and private locations.

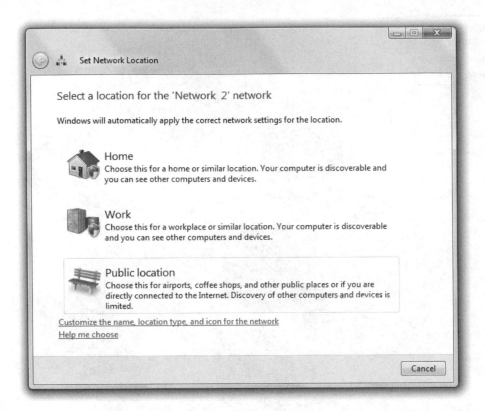

Figure 6-18   Set Network Location in Vista

NOTE   You need Administrator privileges to change the network location in Windows Vista and Windows 7.

Network Location—It's the Firewall!

So what exactly does Windows do when you select Private or Public? Windows configures the Windows Firewall to block or unblock discovery and sharing services. When running on a Private network, Windows enables Network Discovery and File and Printer Sharing as exceptions. When running on a Public network, Windows disables these exceptions.

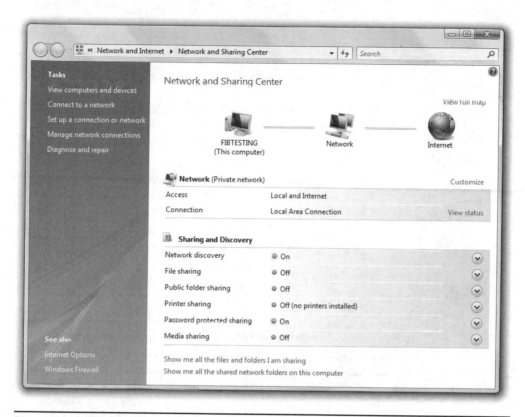

Figure 6-19 The Customize link

EXAM TIP The Network Discovery setting dictates whether your computer can find other computers or devices on a network and vice-versa. Even with Network Discovery activated, several firewall settings can overrule certain connections.

Look at Figure 6-21. Notice that Network Discovery and File and Printer Sharing are currently not checked. This means these exceptions are not enabled. We know this system considers its current network to be a Public network.

In Windows Vista, Microsoft cleverly used Windows Firewall to turn services on and off, but Microsoft made one mistake: the firewall configuration remained the same for every connection. If your Windows machine never changed networks, you wouldn't

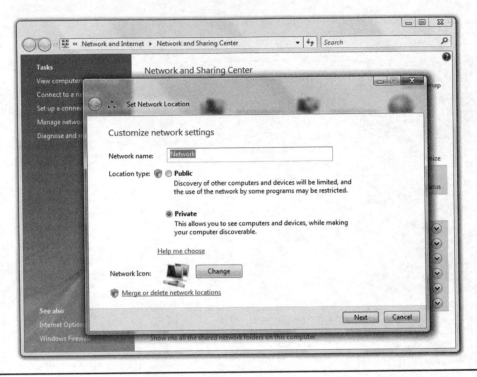

Figure 6-20   Set Network Location

Figure 6-21
Windows Firewall
exceptions

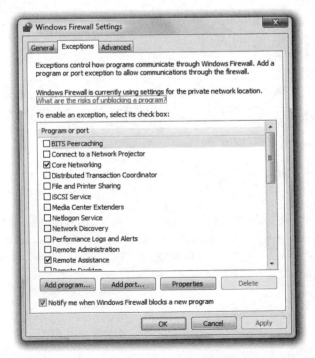

Figure 6-22
Many machines
need more than
one network
setting.

have a problem. But what about machines (mainly laptops) that hop from one network to another (Figure 6-22)? In that case, you need different firewall settings for each network the system might encounter.

In this regard, Windows 7 makes a big departure from Windows Vista. In Windows 7, the Set Network Location dialog box appears every time you connect to a new network (Figure 6-23). Take a moment and compare Figure 6-23 to Figure 6-18.

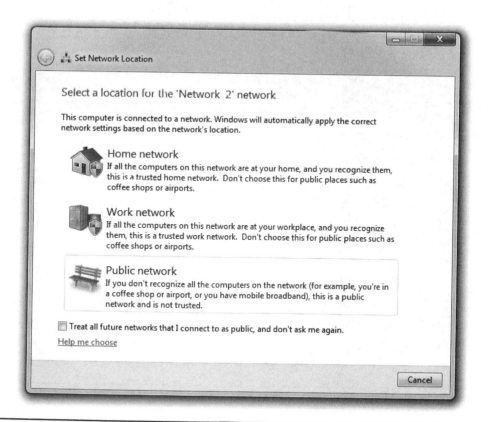

Figure 6-23 Windows 7 Network Location screen

EXAM TIP To change your network location at any time in Windows 7, open the Network and Sharing Center in Control Panel, and then click the link listed under *View your active networks* (the link will be labeled with your current network location). From the dialog box that opens, you can choose a Home, Work, or Public network.

In Windows Vista, you usually saw this screen only once. From then on, any new connection simply took on the Domain/Public/Private settings of the first network connection. In Windows 7, this screen pops up *every time* you encounter a new network. Windows 7, therefore, includes a more complex firewall. Figure 6-24 shows the default Windows Firewall Control Panel applet in Windows Vista.

Figure 6-25 shows the default Windows Firewall applet in Windows 7. Notice that Windows 7 comes with three different firewall settings: one for Domains, one for Private networks (Home or Work), and one for Public networks.

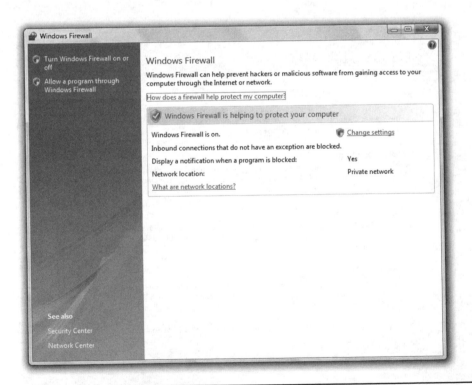

Figure 6-24 Windows Firewall applet in Windows Vista

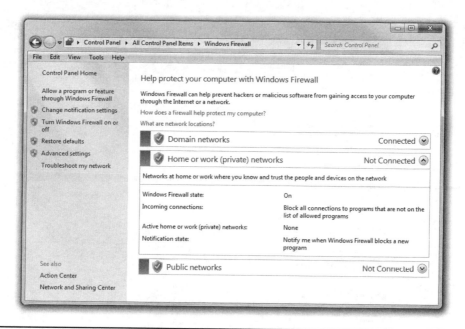

Figure 6-25 Windows Firewall applet in Windows 7

If you click the Advanced Settings option, as shown on the left side of the dialog box in Figure 6-25, you'll discover a much deeper level of firewall configuration, one very different from the settings found in Windows XP (Figure 6-26).

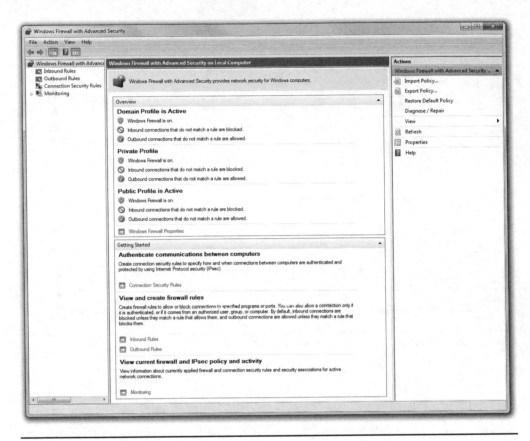

Figure 6-26 Windows Firewall with Advanced Security

Microsoft changed the way Windows treats exceptions. Back in Windows XP, you just chose a program and made it an exception, giving it permission to pass through the firewall. But programs both send and receive network data, so XP ignored the "inbound" and "outbound" aspect of firewalls. Windows 7 takes the exceptions concept and expands it to include rules for both inbound and outbound data. Figure 6-27 shows the outbound rules for a typical Windows 7 system.

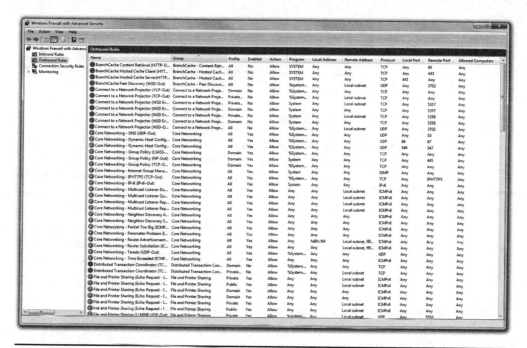

Figure 6-27   Outbound Rules

 NOTE   Windows Vista also includes inbound/outbound rules.

A rule always includes at least the following:

- The name of the program
- Group: an organizational group that helps sort all the rules
- The associated profile (All, Domain, Public, Private)
- Enabled/disabled status
- Remote and local address
- Remote and local port number

Outstanding! With Windows 7's firewall, you get a number of new tools. First, you get a far more powerful form of exceptions. Network locations can turn File Sharing and Discovery on and off. With premade folders, you have a good chance of knowing where people put data. To finish it off, Windows 7 needed a tool for sharing stuff. Microsoft did this with a bit of magic called HomeGroup.

HomeGroup

Finally, after a lengthy explanation, we get to one of the coolest parts of Windows 7— HomeGroup. A homegroup connects a group of computers using a common password. One computer on a network creates a homegroup and generates a password. Every other computer on that network can join that homegroup (if the user enters the password on his or her computer). Let's make a homegroup and watch all this work.

 EXAM TIP Microsoft refers the technology as HomeGroup, but drops the capitalization to homegroup when talking about the groups themselves. Look for it either way on the CompTIA A+ exams.

You make a homegroup by accessing the HomeGroup Control Panel applet. Figure 6-28 shows this applet in the Control Panel. If you can't see this applet, set your Control Panel view to Small or Large icons.

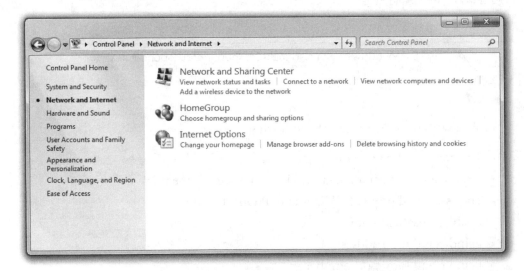

Figure 6-28 Network and Internet category in Windows 7 Control Panel

Assuming you connect to a workgroup (not a domain) on a Home network, have IPv6 running (HomeGroup only runs on IPv6—cool!), and have not already created a homegroup, you'll see a dialog box like the one in Figure 6-29 when you open the HomeGroup Control Panel applet.

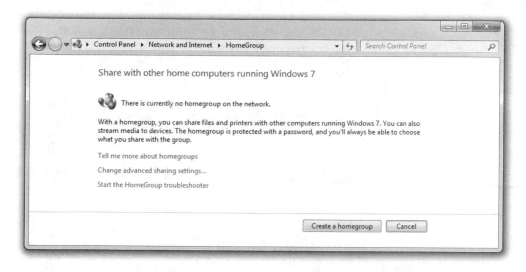

Figure 6-29   Default HomeGroup dialog box

Click the *Create a homegroup* button to create a homegroup. You'll then see another dialog box (Figure 6-30).

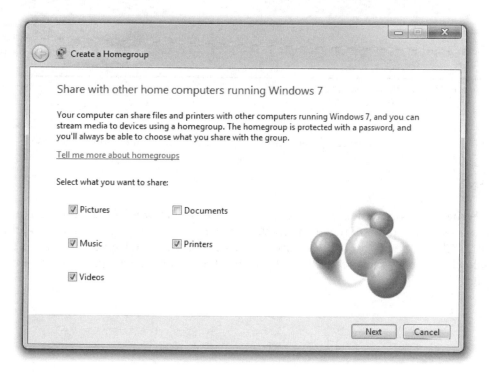

Figure 6-30   Create a Homegroup dialog box

Notice the five options: Pictures, Music, Videos, Documents, and Printers. The Documents checkbox is probably not checked, but go ahead and check it to share all five things. Click Next to see the homegroup's password (Figure 6-31)

Figure 6-31 The homegroup's password

 NOTE Interestingly, all homegroup data is encrypted between systems.

Perhaps you've heard that you shouldn't write down passwords? Well, this password is so long you might *need* to write it down. The dialog box even gives you a way to print it out! Click Next one more time to see the dialog box shown in Figure 6-32. This is the dialog box you will now see every time you click the HomeGroup applet in the Control Panel.

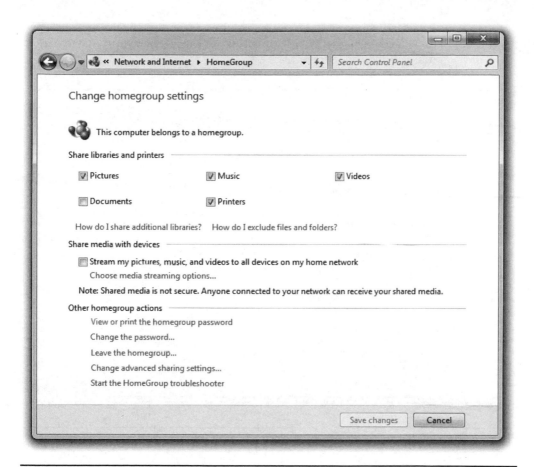

Figure 6-32   Homegroup configured

Let's look at this carefully. Notice where it says *Share libraries and printers* and, a bit lower, *How do I share additional libraries?* By default, homegroups share libraries, not individual folders. The Music, Pictures, Videos, and Documents libraries are shared by default—the four default libraries mentioned back in Chapter 1. Although printers get their own checkbox, this setting remains the same as a normal printer share. It's just a handy place to add printer sharing, as even the most basic users like to share printers.

EXAM TIP   Remember that homegroups share libraries, not folders, by default.

Once you've created a homegroup, go to another computer on the network and open up the HomeGroup Control Panel applet. Assuming all the factors stated earlier, you will see a dialog box like Figure 6-33.

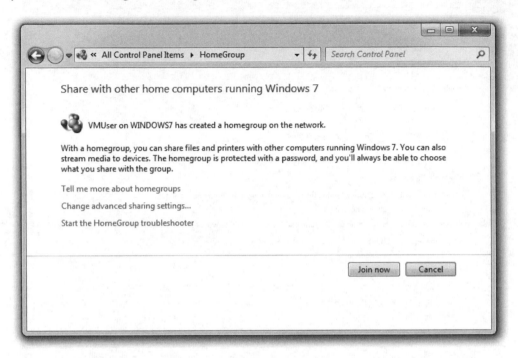

Figure 6-33 HomeGroup showing an existing homegroup

Click the Join Now button, enter the password, choose which libraries you want to share with everyone else, and the new computer is in the homegroup! All user accounts on the computer you add become members of the homegroup.

Access the files shared through a homegroup by opening up Windows Explorer, as shown in Figure 6-34. To see what others are sharing, select the corresponding computer name. You can then open those libraries to see the shared folders.

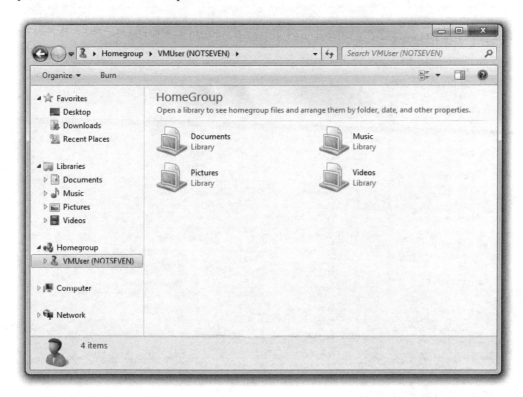

Figure 6-34   Using homegroups

 NOTE   Once you create a homegroup, you can access it from Windows Explorer.

Sharing more libraries is easy, and, if you'd like, you can even share individual folders. Just right-click on the library or folder and select Share With, as shown in Figure 6-35.

Figure 6-35 The Share with menu

Notice you have four options: *Nobody* (the item is not shared), *Homegroup Read*, *Homegroup Read/Write*, and *Specific people*.

 EXAM TIP Windows Explorer also adds a Share with toolbar button that works exactly like Figure 6-35.

The Specific people option is interesting. Select it and you'll see a screen you've seen before (Figure 6-36).

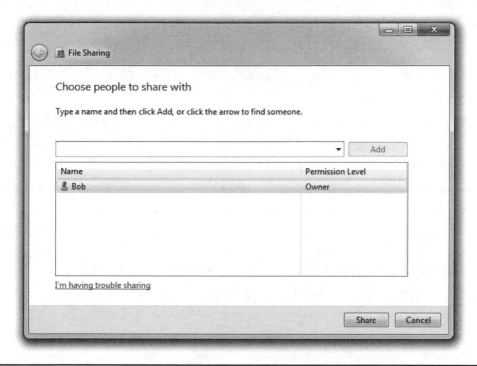

Figure 6-36 Windows 7 File Sharing Wizard

Yup, it's the good old File Sharing Wizard, just like in Windows Vista. You have to hand it to Microsoft on this one—it almost seamlessly ties homegroups into the old File Sharing Wizard.

By sharing libraries with homegroups, Microsoft hides folders for most users, helping users share their stuff (documents, pictures, music, and movies) instead of folders. Homegroups fit a very specific world: smaller, nondomain home networks, but within that realm, they work wonderfully.

Windows 7—The Best of All Worlds?

To appreciate the power of Windows 7 networks, you need to understand how earlier versions of Windows handled networking. Whereas Windows 2000 only supported classic network shares with NTFS, Windows XP introduced Simple File Sharing. Windows Vista expanded this with robust IPv6, network discovery, and network location features. Windows 7 merely adds the concept of homegroups while still fully supporting both Vista's File Sharing Wizard and even full-blown, old school NTFS sharing.

Chapter Review

Questions

1. Which of the following sharing tools did Windows XP introduce?

    A. File Sharing Wizard

    B. NTFS permissions

    C. Simple File Sharing

    D. HomeGroup

2. What can a Contributor do with shared files in Windows Vista?

    A. View or add files to the shared folder but can only alter or delete files he or she has contributed

    B. Do anything to the shared folder or anything in the shared folder

    C. View shared files, but not change them or delete them

    D. View, add, alter, or delete any shared file

3. In Windows 7, which of the following network locations enable you to discover other devices on a network?

    A. Home

    B. Work

    C. Public

    D. Private

4. When setting a network location, why can you not choose Domain?

    A. Domains do not affect your network location.

    B. Both public and private networks can be used on domains.

    C. If you are on a domain, you won't be prompted to pick a network location at all.

    D. Domains are only used on network locations with homegroups.

5. Which of the following security features is affected by network location?

    A. User Account Control

    B. Windows Defender

    C. Windows Firewall

    D. BitLocker

6. Which of the following is required to create a homegroup? (Select two.)

   A. A workgroup

   B. IPv6

   C. An Internet connection

   D. Shared folders

7. Which of the following technologies is *not* a part of Microsoft's Rally?

   A. IPv6

   B. UPnP

   C. qWave

   D. LLTD

8. Which of the following situations could benefit most from implementing a homegroup?

   A. A large corporation where hundreds of employees need access to the same files

   B. A home with a single computer

   C. A small business that shares files back and forth between a few computers

   D. A network of computers using a domain controller

9. Which of the following libraries is not shared on a homegroup by default?

   A. Documents

   B. Pictures

   C. Music

   D. Videos

10. Which operating system most recently included the File Sharing Wizard?

    A. Windows 2000

    B. Windows XP

    C. Windows Vista

    D. Windows 7

Answers

1. **C.** Windows XP introduced Simple File Sharing to help users who had trouble dealing with NTFS permissions.

2. **A.** A Contributor can view or add files to the shared folder but can only alter or delete files he or she has contributed.

3. **D.** Private networks enable your computer to discover other devices.

4. **C.** When joining a domain network, you do not need to pick whether it is a private or public network.

5. **C.** Network locations adjust your firewall depending on what type of network you connect to.

6. **A, B.** Setting up a homegroup requires being a member of a workgroup and using IPv6.

7. **A.** Microsoft Rally includes UPnP, qWave, and LLTD.

8. **C.** Homegroups are best when implemented using a few trusted computers.

9. **A.** The Documents library is not shared by default on a homegroup.

10. **D.** The File Sharing Wizard can still be used in Windows 7 (though you would probably be happier using homegroups).

CHAPTER 7

Windows 7 Utilities

This chapter ties into what you learned from

- **All-In-One:** Chapter 17
- **Managing and Troubleshooting:** Chapter 17
- **Meyers' Guide to 702:** Chapter 8

Windows 7 includes amazing new utilities designed to help you support your system. Many of these first appeared in Windows Vista, but Windows 7 either refined them or made them easily accessible. These tools perform a number of different jobs, from telling you what's happening on the system to showing you how well your system's performance stacks up to other computers.

Although these utilities are all different, you can find all of them in the Control Panel. Action Center centralizes a lot of useful information about the status of your computer. BitLocker Drive Encryption keeps your files under lock and key. Windows 7's Event Viewer makes a great troubleshooting tool even better, while the Performance and Information Tools applet tells you just how powerful your computer really is. Let's take a look at this crazy mixture of utilities in alphabetical order.

Action Center

Sometimes, you just want to glance at your system and know that nothing has gone terribly wrong. Previous versions of Windows lacked a single "peephole" to view the status of your computer. Action Center fills that gap, providing a one-page aggregation of event messages, warnings, and maintenance messages that, for many techs, might quickly replace Event Viewer as the first place to look for problems. Unlike Event Viewer, the Action Center separates issues into two sections, Security and Maintenance, making it easier to scan a system quickly (Figure 7-1).

Action Center only compiles the information, taking data from well-known utilities such as Event Viewer, Windows Update, Windows Firewall, and UAC and places it into an easy-to-read format. If you wish, you can tell Action Center where to look for information by selecting *Change Action Center settings* (Figure 7-2).

If you see a problem, Action Center includes plenty of links to get you to the utility you need. From the Action Center applet, you get direct links to

- UAC settings
- Performance Information and Tools
- Backup and Restore
- Windows Update
- Troubleshooting Wizard
- System Restore

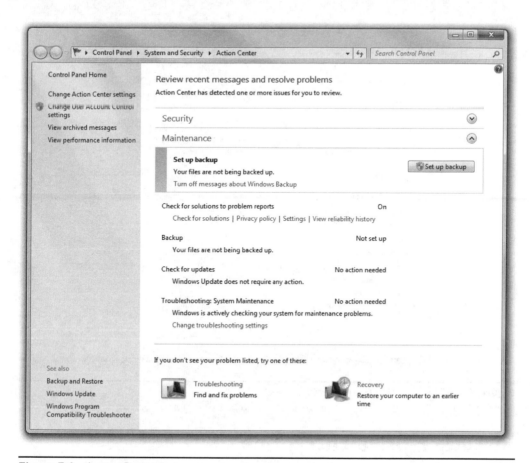

Figure 7-1 Action Center

Although Action Center does little more than reproduce information from other utilities, it makes finding problems quick and easy. Combined with quick links to most of the utilities you'll need, Action Center should become your base of operations when something goes wrong on your PC.

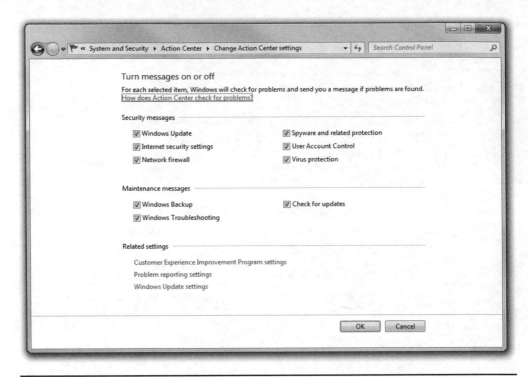

Figure 7-2   Change Action Center settings

BitLocker Drive Encryption

Microsoft introduced the powerful BitLocker Drive Encryption tool with Windows Vista and refined it in Windows 7. To use BitLocker to encrypt your hard drives, you need two things: a motherboard with a Trusted Platform Module (TPM) chip and at least two partitions.

TPM provides a fixed encryption key on a chip. You can use this key in a number of ways. You can associate hardware to a specific motherboard, creating a way to authenticate hardware with a particular motherboard. You can also use the key for encryption using BitLocker. Figure 7-3 shows a typical TPM chip on a modern motherboard.

I need to come clean on one issue. Although the CompTIA A+ exams may tell you that you need a TPM chip, Windows 7 enables you to use BitLocker on a motherboard without a TPM chip. Instead, you can use a USB drive to store the key. To do this, you need to open up the Local Group Policy Editor. Go to a command prompt and type **GPEDIT.MSC**. Navigate down the menu on the left like so: Computer Configuration | Administrative Templates | Windows Components | BitLocker Drive Encryption | Operating System Drives. Then double-click *Require additional authentication at startup* and select *Enabled* (Figure 7-4). Be warned. If you ever lose the USB drive that stores the key, you'll probably lose all the data on the drive.

Figure 7-3 TPM chip

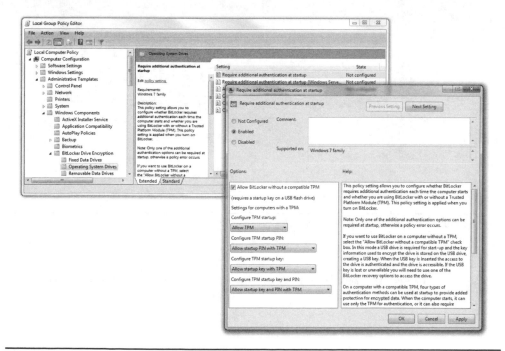

Figure 7-4 Using GPEDIT to skip over the TPM requirement

Assuming your computer meets the requirements, you can easily set up BitLocker. From the BitLocker Drive Encryption applet, click Turn on BitLocker to start the wizard. It connects to your TPM, creates a partition, prompts for the drive to encrypt (unless you only have one), and sets everything up. It even gives you the option to choose the drive to encrypt if you have more than one. Finally, BitLocker gives you the ability to save a backup (recovery) key in case something goes wrong with your motherboard (Figure 7-5).

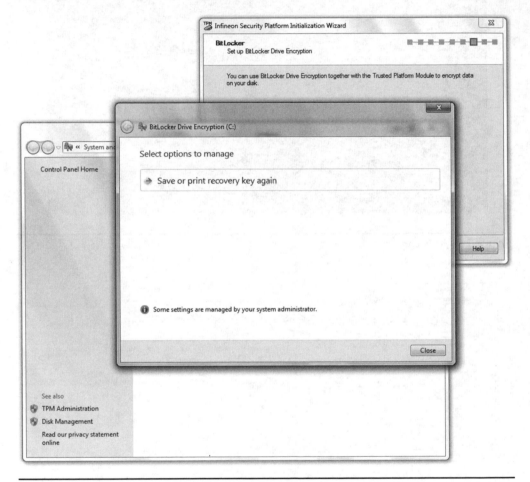

Figure 7-5 BitLocker prompts you to save a recovery key

 EXAM TIP BitLocker in Windows Vista requires you to create a second partition manually. Windows 7 creates the partition automatically.

BitLocker has a few rules:

- Only the Ultimate and Enterprise editions of Windows Vista and Windows 7 include BitLocker.

- BitLocker will not encrypt dynamic drives.

- BitLocker will only encrypt secondary drives if the drive storing the OS is already encrypted with BitLocker.

- BitLocker is not the same as the Encrypting File System! BitLocker encrypts entire volumes; EFS encrypts as little as a single file.

- This is my own rule: Always make a recovery key. If the motherboard fails, you have no other way to recover the data.

Microsoft added a new feature to Windows 7's version of BitLocker called BitLocker to Go. BitLocker to Go encrypts removable drives, a great way to encrypt your USB thumb drives or eSATA drives. BitLocker to Go doesn't require a TPM chip, either.

Depending on your situation, encrypting your entire hard drive with BitLocker might seem like overkill. Even with all of its power, though, BitLocker Drive Encryption adds an easy to use layer of security for all of your system's data.

Event Viewer

I covered Event Viewer in the main text, so why bring it up again? Well, Windows 7 adds an easy-to-use interface to Event Viewer (while retaining the old Windows XP style if you prefer it). Opening Event Viewer (System and Security | Administrative Tools | Event Viewer) shows you a very different interface than the one you've seen in Windows XP (Figure 7-6).

Note the four main bars: Overview, Summary of Administrative Events, Recently Viewed Nodes, and Log Summary. Pay special attention to the Summary of Administrative Events. It breaks down the events into different levels: Critical, Error, Warning, Information, Audit Success, and Audit Failure. Figure 7-7 shows a typical Summary with the Warning Events opened. You can then click any event to see a dialog describing the event in detail. Microsoft refers to these as *Views*.

Windows 7's Event Viewer still includes the classic logs you saw in Windows XP (Application, Security, and System) but leans heavily on Views to show you the contents of the logs. Views filter existing log files, making them great for custom reports using beginning/end times, levels of errors, and more. You can use the built-in Views or easily create custom Views, as shown in Figure 7-8.

 NOTE By default, Event Viewer stores logs as .evtx files in the C:\ WINDOWS\SYSTEM32\WINEVT\LOGS folder.

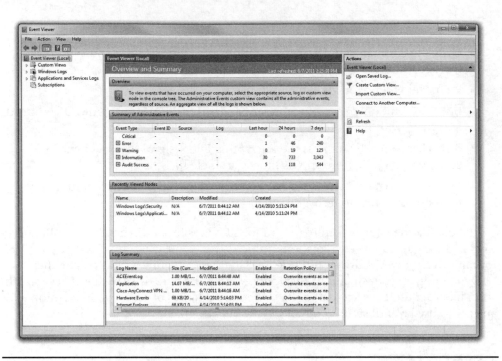

Figure 7-6 Event Viewer default screen

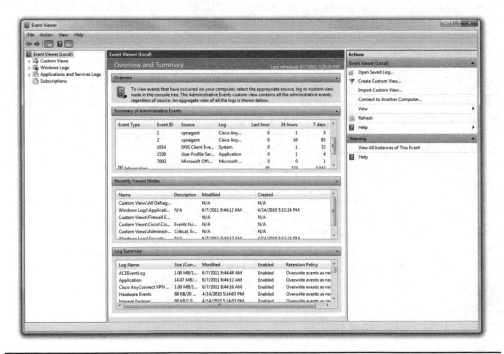

Figure 7-7 Warning Events open

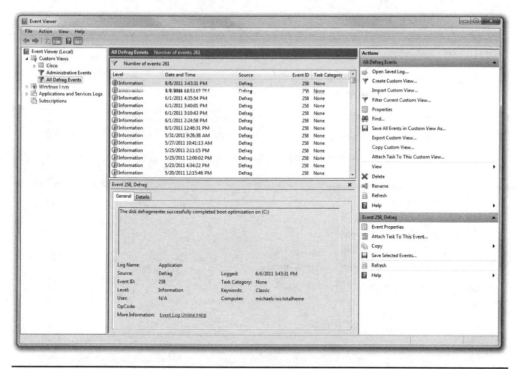

Figure 7-8　Create Custom Views

Remember, you still record all data to logs. Logs in Windows 7 still have the same limitations that logs in earlier versions of Windows had. They have a maximum size, a location, and a behavior for when they get too big (such as overwrite the log or make an error). Figure 7-9 shows a typical Log Properties dialog box in Windows 7.

EXAM TIP　Only users with Administrator privileges can make changes to log files in Event Viewer.

Windows 7's Event Viewer remains largely untouched in terms of the data collected, but Microsoft did a great job of making that data much easier to understand and use.

Performance Information and Tools

Techs must often answer difficult questions like "Why is my machine running so slowly?" Before Windows Vista, we could only use Performance Monitor baselines or third-party tools. Neither of these options worked very well. Baselines required you to choose the right counters—choosing the wrong counters made useless and sometimes even distracting logs. Third-party tools often measured one aspect of a system

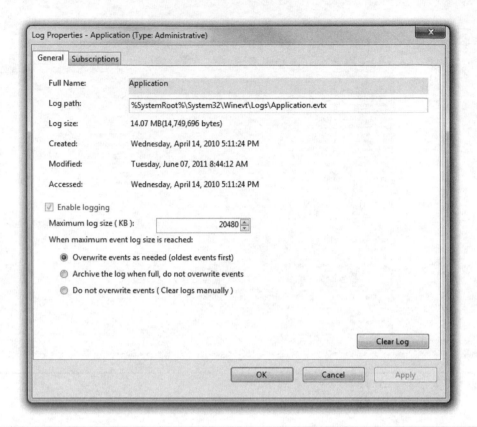

Figure 7-9   Log Properties in Windows 7

(like video quality) very well but didn't help much when you wanted an overview of your system.

This changed with Microsoft's introduction of the Performance Information and Tools Control Panel applet (Figure 7-10).

 EXAM TIP   Find the Performance Information and Tools applet from Control Panel's Category view by clicking System and Security | Check the Windows Experience Index.

The Performance Information and Tools applet doesn't fix anything. It just provides a relative feel for how your computer stacks up against other systems using the Windows Experience Index. Windows bases this on five components:

- **Processor**   Calculations per second
- **Memory (RAM)**   Memory operations per second

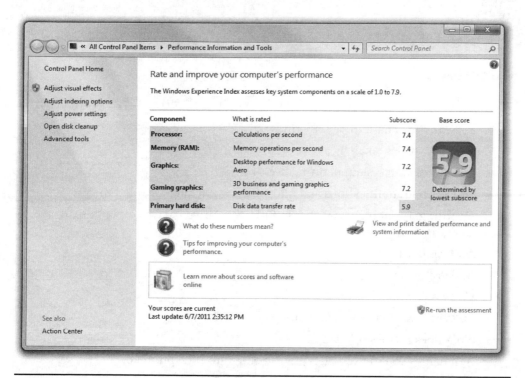

Figure 7-10 Performance Information and Tools

- **Graphics**   Desktop performance for Windows Aero
- **Gaming Graphics**   3-D business and gaming graphics performance
- **Primary hard disk**   Disk data transfer rate

Each component generates a subscore. These values range from 1 to 5.9 for Windows Vista and 1 to 7.9 for Windows 7. Microsoft determines the calculations that generate these numbers, so I don't know exactly what it takes to give, for example, a CPU a score of 6.1. Your system's Base score is based on the lowest subscore.

The Performance Information and Tools applet won't fix any one problem a PC has, but it's a great indicator of the power of a computer. If a computer feels sluggish overall, check the Windows Experience Index to see where it ranks—it might surprise you.

EXAM TIP   You can't change a subscore in the Windows Experience Index without making some kind of hardware change.

Chapter Review

Questions

1. What does the Action Center do?

    A. Scans your hard drive for viruses

    B. Logs actions taken by a user on the computer

    C. Grades your system performance

    D. Compiles notifications and information generated by other tools

2. According to CompTIA, what does BitLocker Drive Encryption require to function? (Select two.)

    A. 1 TB hard drive

    B. TPM device

    C. Two partitions

    D. Windows 7 Professional Edition

3. What does BitLocker to Go do?

    A. Enables you to use a USB drive to store the encryption key

    B. Enables you to encrypt USB drives using BitLocker

    C. Enables you to take a TPM from one motherboard and use it on another

    D. Enables you to back up your encryption key

4. In Event Viewer, what are Views?

    A. Views replaced the logs from Windows XP.

    B. Views filter existing logs into reports.

    C. Views change how logs are recorded.

    D. Views have nothing to do with Event Viewer.

5. How is the base score of your Windows Experience Index determined?

    A. It is an average of all six subscores.

    B. It is the highest subscore.

    C. It is the lowest subscore.

    D. It is the average of your Processor, Memory, and Primary Hard Disk subscores.

6. You set up BitLocker Drive Encryption on your computer using a USB drive to store the key. You don't bother to make a backup of the key. You then lose the USB drive. How do you retrieve the encrypted data?

   A. Plug the hard drive into a different TPM-enabled motherboard and redo the BitLocker setup.

   B. Restore your computer to a time before you lost the USB key and attempt to access your drive.

   C. You cannot retrieve the data without the key.

   D. Run Disk Defragmenter to decrypt the data.

7. Which Control Panel category contains Administrative Tools?

   A. System and Security

   B. Network and Internet

   C. Hardware and Sound

   D. Appearance and Personalization

8. What does TPM stand for?

   A. True Performance Meter

   B. Trusted Performance Measure

   C. Trusted Platform Meter

   D. Trusted Platform Module

9. What path do you follow to reach the Performance Information and Tools in Category view?

   A. Start | Accessories | System Tools | Performance Information and Tools

   B. Start | Control Panel | Hardware and Sound | Performance Information and Tools

   C. Start | Control Panel | System and Security | Check the Windows Experience Index

   D. Start | Control Panel | System and Security | Performance Information and Tools

10. What type of account can make changes to log files in Event Viewer?

    A. Administrator

    B. Standard user

    C. Guest

    D. You cannot change log files at all.

Answers

1. **D.** The Action Center compiles information from other tools and utilities and shows it all in a single location.

2. **B, C.** BitLocker Drive Encryption (according to the CompTIA A+ exams) requires two partitions and a TPM-enabled motherboard.

3. **B.** BitLocker to Go enables you to encrypt a USB drive.

4. **B.** In Event Viewer, Views filter existing logs into reports.

5. **C.** Your Windows Experience Index base score is determined by the lowest subscore.

6. **C.** Sadly, you most likely cannot retrieve the data without the key on the USB drive.

7. **A.** Administrative tools can be found in the System and Security category of Control Panel.

8. **D.** TPM stands for Trusted Platform Module.

9. **C.** You can find the Performance Information and Tools applet by going to Start | Control Panel | System and Security | Check the Windows Experience Index.

10. **A.** Only Administrator accounts can make changes to Event Viewer logs.

Mapping to the CompTIA A+ Objectives

The new 2011 exam objectives add a lot of content to both CompTIA A+ exams. To help you understand where the new material fits into the exams, I've included a map of the new and old objectives with references to corresponding chapters in *CompTIA A+ Certification All-in-One Exam Guide, Mike Meyers' CompTIA A+ Guide to Managing and Troubleshooting PCs*, as well as this book (indicated by *Win 7* in the following tables). Use this map to find where I covered each objective in all three books.

NOTE *Mike Meyers' CompTIA A+ Guide to Managing and Troubleshooting PCs* and *CompTIA A+ Certification All-in-One Exam Guide* use the same chapter numbers in the following objective map.

CompTIA A+ Essentials Objectives Map

Topic	Chapter(s)
Domain 1.0 Hardware	
1.1 Categorize storage devices and backup media	
FDD	3
HDD	3, 11
Solid state vs. magnetic	11
Optical drives	3, 13
CD / DVD / RW / Blu-ray	3, 13
Removable storage	11, 13, 17
Tape drive	17
Solid state (e.g. thumb drive, flash, SD cards, USB)	13
External CD-RW and hard drive	13, 11
Hot swappable devices and non-hot swappable devices	13
1.2 Explain motherboard components, types and features	
Form Factor	9
ATX / BTX	9
micro ATX	9
NLX	9
I/O interfaces	3, 18, 20, 22, 23, 25
Sound	3, 20
Video	3
USB 1.1 and 2.0	3, 18
Serial	3, 18

Topic	Chapter(s)
IEEE 1394 / Firewire	3, 18
Parallel	3, 22
NIC	3, 23
Modem	3, 25
PS/2	18
Memory slots	3, 6
RIMM	6
DIMM	3, 6
SODIMM	6
SIMM	6
Processor sockets	3, 5, 9
Bus architecture	5, 8
Bus slots	8, 9, 21
PCI	8, 9
AGP	8, 9
PCIe	8, 9
AMR	9
CNR	9
PCMCIA	21
PATA	11
IDE	11
EIDE	11
SATA, eSATA	3, 11
Contrast RAID (levels 0, 1, 5)	11, 12
Chipsets	5, 7, 9
BIOS / CMOS / Firmware	7
POST	7
CMOS battery	7
Riser card / daughterboard	9
1.3 Classify power supplies types and characteristics	
AC adapter	10
ATX proprietary	10
Voltage, wattage, and capacity	10
Voltage selector switch	10
Pins (20, 24)	10

Topic	Chapter(s)
1.4 Explain the purpose and characteristics of CPUs and their features	
Identify CPU types	5
AMD	5
Intel	5
Hyper threading	5
Multi core	5
Dual core	5
Triple core	5
Quad core	5
Onchip cache	5
L1	5
L2	5
Speed (real vs. actual)	5
32 bit vs. 64 bit	5
1.5 Explain cooling methods and devices	
Heat sinks	5
CPU and case fans	5, 10
Liquid cooling systems	5
Thermal compound	5
1.6 Compare and contrast memory types, characteristics, and their purpose	
Types	5, 6
DRAM	5, 6
SRAM	5
SDRAM	6
DDR / DDR2 / DDR3	6
RDRAM	6
Parity vs. Non-parity	6
ECC vs. non-ECC	6
Single sided vs. double sided	6
Single channel vs. dual channel	6
Speed	6
PC100	6
PC133	6

Topic	Chapter(s)
PC2700	6
PC3200	6
DDR3-1600	6
DDR2-667	6

1.7 Distinguish between the different display devices and their characteristics

Topic	Chapter(s)
Projectors, CRT and LCD	19
LCD technologies	19
Resolution (e.g. XGA, SXGA+, UXGA, WUXGA)	19
Contrast ratio	19
Native resolution	19
Connector types	3, 19
VGA	3, 19
HDMi	3, 19
S-Video	19
Component / RGB	19
DVI pin compatibility	19
Settings	19
Refresh rate	19
Resolution	19
Multi-monitor	19
Degauss	19

1.8 Install and configure peripherals and input devices

Topic	Chapter(s)
Mouse	18
Keyboard	18
Bar code reader	18
Multimedia (e.g. web and digital cameras, MIDI, microphones)	18
Biometric devices	18
Touch screen	18
KVM switch	18

1.9 Summarize the function and types of adapter cards

Topic	Chapter(s)
Video	8, 19
PCI	8, 19
PCIe	8, 19
AGP	8, 19

Topic	Chapter(s)
Multimedia	20
Sound card	20
TV tuner cards	20
Capture cards	20
I/O	3, 11, 18, 22
SCSI	3, 11
Serial	3, 18
USB	3, 18
Parallel	3, 22
Communications	3, 23
NIC	23
Modem	23
1.10 Install, configure, and optimize laptop components and features	
Expansion devices	21
PCMCIA cards	21
PCI Express cards	21
Docking station	21
Communication connections	21, 23, 24, 25
Bluetooth	21, 24
Infrared	21, 24
Cellular WAN	21, 24
Ethernet	21, 23
Modem	21, 25
Power and electrical input devices	10, 21
Auto-switching	10
Fixed input power supplies	10
Batteries	21
Input devices	21
Stylus / digitizer	21
Function keys	21
Point devices (e.g. touch pad, point stick / track point)	21

Topic	Chapter(s)
1.11 Install and configure printers	
Differentiate between printer types	22
Laser	22
Inkjet	22
Thermal	22
Impact	22
Local vs. network printers	22
Printer drivers (compatibility)	22
Consumables	22
Domain 2.0 Troubleshooting, Repair, and Maintenance	
2.1 Given a scenario, explain the troubleshooting theory	
Identify the problem	23, 27
Question the user and identify user changes to computer and perform backups before making changes	23, 27
Establish a theory of probable cause (question the obvious)	23, 27
Test the theory to determine cause	23, 27
Once theory is confirmed determine next steps to resolve problem	27
If theory is not confirmed re-establish new theory or escalate	27
Establish a plan of action to resolve the problem and implement the solution	27
Verify full system functionality and if applicable implement preventative measures	27
Document findings, actions, and outcomes	27
2.2 Given a scenario, explain and interpret common hardware and operating system symptoms and their causes	
OS related symptoms	4, 6, 9, 10, 17, 18, 22
Bluescreen	6, 9, 17
System lock-up	6, 10, 17
Input / output device	18
Application install	4
Start or load	17
Windows specific printing problems	22
Print spool stalled	22
Incorrect / incompatible driver	22

Topic	Chapter(s)
Hardware related symptoms	5, 6, 8, 10, 12, 13, 19, 23, 27
Excessive heat	5, 10, 27
Noise	5, 12, 27
Odors	13, 27
Status light indicators	23
Alerts	5, 6, 8, 10, 17
Visible damage (e.g. cable, plastic)	5, 23, 27
Use documentation and resources	12, 17, 22
User / installation manuals	22
Internet / Web based	12
Training materials	17

2.3 Given a scenario, determine the troubleshooting methods and tools for printers

Manage print jobs	22
Print spooler	22
Printer properties and settings	22
Print a test page	22

2.4 Given a scenario, explain and interpret common laptop issues and determine the appropriate basic troubleshooting method

Issues	21
Power conditions	21
Video	21
Keyboard	21
Pointer	21
Stylus	21
Wireless card issues	21
Methods	10, 21
Verify power (e.g. LEDs, swap AC adapter)	10, 21
Remove unneeded peripherals	21
Plug in external monitor	21
Toggle Fn keys or hardware switches	21
Check LCD cutoff switch	21
Verify backlight functionality and pixelation	21
Check switch for built-in Wi-Fi antennas or external antennas	21

Topic	Chapter(s)
2.5 Given a scenario, integrate common preventative maintenance techniques	
Physical inspection	5, 11, 12, 22
Updates	4, 17
Driver	8, 17
Firmware	7
OS	17
Security	16, 26
Scheduling preventative maintenance	4, 17
Defrag	17
Scandisk	17
Check disk	17
Startup programs	4, 17
Use of appropriate repair tools and cleaning materials	5, 19, 21, 22
Compressed air	21, 22
Lint free cloth	19
Computer vacuum and compressors	5
Power devices	10
Appropriate source such as power strip, surge protector, or UPS	10
Ensuring proper environment	21
Backup procedures	16
Domain 3.0 Operating Systems and Software – Unless otherwise noted, operating systems referred to within include Microsoft Windows 2000, Windows XP Professional, XP Home, XP MediaCenter, Windows Vista Home, Home Premium, Business and Ultimate, *Windows 7 Starter, Home Premium, Professional, and Ultimate*	
3.1 Compare and contrast the different Windows Operating Systems and their features	
Windows 2000, Windows XP 32 bit vs. 64 bit, Windows Vista 32 bit vs. 64 bit, *Windows 7 32 bit vs. 64 bit*	4, 5, *Win 7: 1*
Sidebar, Aero, UAC, minimum system requirements, system limits	4, *Win 7: 1, 2, 4*
Windows 2000 and newer – upgrade paths and requirements	14, *Win 7: 2*
Windows OS Upgrade Advisor	*Win 7: 2*
Microsoft Assessment and Planning Toolkit	*Win 7: 2*
Terminology (32 bit vs. 64 bit – ×86 vs. ×64)	4, 5, *Win 7: 2*
Application compatibility, installed program locations (32 bit vs. 64 bit), Windows compatibility mode	4, *Win 7: 2*
User interface, start bar layout	4, *Win 7: 1*

Topic	Chapter(s)
3.2 Given a scenario, demonstrate proper use of user interfaces	
Windows Explorer	4, *Win 7: 1*
Libraries in Windows 7	*Win 7: 1*
My Computer	4
Control Panel	4, *Win 7: 7*
Command prompt utilities	15, *Win 7: 2*
telnet	25
ping	23, 25
ipconfig	23, 25
Run line utilities	4, 15, 17, 19
msconfig	17
msinfo32	17
Dxdiag	19
Cmd	4, 15
REGEDIT	4
My Network Places	4
Task bar / systray	4, *Win 7: 1*
Administrative tools	4, 17, 26
Performance monitor, Event Viewer, Services, Computer Management	4, 17, 26, *Win 7: 7*
MMC	4
Task Manager	17
Start Menu	4
3.3 Explain the process and steps to install and configure the Windows OS	
File systems	12, 14
FAT32 vs. NTFS	4, 12, 14, 16
Directory structures	4, 14, 15
Create folders	15
Navigate directory structures	4, 15
Files	4, 14
Creation	14
Extensions	4, 15, 20
Attributes	15
Permissions	16

Topic	Chapter(s)
Verification of hardware compatibility and minimum requirements	14
Installation methods	14
Boot media such as CD, floppy, or USB	13, 14
Network installation	14
Install from image	14
Recover CD	17
Factory recovery partition	17
Operating system installation options	12, 14
File system type	12, 14
Network configuration	14
Repair install	14
Disk preparation order	12, 14
Format drive	12, 14
Partition	12, 14
Start installation	12, 14
Device Manager	4, 7, 8
Verify	8
Install and update devices drivers	8
Driver signing	8, 17
User data migration – User State Migration Tool (USMT)	14
Virtual memory	4, 8
Configure power management	21
Suspend	21
Wake on LAN	21
Sleep timers	21
Hibernate	21
Standby	21
Demonstrate safe removal of peripherals	3, 21
3.4 Explain the basics of boot sequences, methods, and startup utilities	
Disk boot order / device priority	11
Types of boot devices (disk, network, USB, other)	11

Topic	Chapter(s)
Boot options	15, 17, *Win 7: 3*
Safe mode	15, 17, *Win 7: 3*
Boot to restore point	17
Recovery options	17, *Win 7: 3*
Automated System Recovery (ASR)	17
Emergency Repair Disk (ERD)	17
Recovery console	17
Domain 4.0 Networking	
4.1 Summarize the basics of networking fundamentals, including technologies, devices, and protocols	
Basics of configuring IP addressing and TCP/IP properties (DHCP, DNS)	23
Bandwidth and latency	25
Status indicators	23
Protocols (TCP/IP, NETBIOS)	23
Full-duplex, half-duplex	23
Basics of workgroups and domains	23
Common ports: HTTP, FTP, POP, SMTP, TELNET, HTTPS	25
LAN / WAN	23
Hub, switch, and router	23
Identify Virtual Private Networks (VPN)	25
Basics class identification	23
IPv6 vs. IPv4	*Win 7: 5*
Address length differences	*Win 7: 5*
Address conventions	*Win 7: 5*
4.2 Categorize network cables and connectors and their implementations	
Cables	23
Plenum / PVC	23
UTP (e.g., CAT3, CAT5 / 5e, CAT6)	23
STP	23
Fiber	23
Coaxial cable	23
Connectors	23
RJ45	23
RJ11	23

Topic	Chapter(s)
4.3 Compare and contrast the different network types	
Broadband	25
DSL	25
Cable	25
Satellite	25
Fiber	25
Dial-up	25
Wireless	24
All 802.11 types	24
WEP	24
WPA	24
SSID	24
MAC filtering	24
DHCP settings	24
Bluetooth	24
Cellular	24
Domain 5.0 Security	
5.1 Explain the basic principles of security concepts and technologies	
Encryption technologies	12, 16, 24, 26, *Win 7: 7*
Data wiping / hard drive destruction / hard drive recycling	16
Software firewall	26
Port security	26
Exceptions	26
Authentication technologies	16, 26
User name	16, 26
Password	16, 26
Biometrics	26
Smart cards	26
Basics of data sensitivity and data security	26
Compliance	26
Classifications	26
Social engineering	26

Topic	Chapter(s)
5.2 Summarize the following security features	
Wireless encryption	24
WEPx and WPAx	24
Client configuration (SSID)	24
Malicious software protection	26
Viruses	26
Trojans	26
Worms	26
Spam	26
Spyware	26
Adware	26
Grayware	26
BIOS Security	7, 26
Drive lock	7
Passwords	7, 26
Intrusion detection	7
TPM	7
Password management / password complexity	16, 26
Locking workstation	4, 26
Hardware	26
Operating system	16
Biometrics	26
Fingerprint scanner	26
Domain 6.0 Operational Procedure	
6.1 Outline the purpose of appropriate safety and environmental procedures and, given a scenario, apply them	
ESD	2
EMI	2
Network interference	2
Magnets	2
RFI	2
Cordless phone interference	2
Microwaves	2

Topic	Chapter(s)
Electrical safety	10
CRT	19
Power supply	10
Inverter	19
Laser printers	22
Matching power requirements of equipment with power distribution and UPSs	10
Material Safety Data Sheets (MSDS)	22
Cable management	2
Avoiding trip hazards	2
Physical safety	2
Heavy devices	2
Hot components	2
Environmental – consider proper disposal procedures	22

6.2 Given a scenario, demonstrate the appropriate use of communication skills and professionalism in the workplace

Topic	Chapter(s)
Use proper language – avoid jargon, acronyms, slang	2
Maintain a positive attitude	2
Listen and do not interrupt a customer	2
Be culturally sensitive	2
Be on time	2
If late, contact the customer	2
Avoid distractions	2
Personal calls	2
Talking to co-workers while interacting with customers	2
Personal interruptions	2
Dealing with a difficult customer or situation	2
Avoid arguing with customers and/or being defensive	2
Do not minimize customers' problems	2
Avoid being judgmental	2
Clarify customer statements	2
Ask open-ended questions to narrow the scope of the problem	2
Restate the issue or question to verify understanding	2

Topic	Chapter(s)
Set and meet expectations / timeline and communicate status with the customer	2
Offer different repair / replacement options if applicable	2
Provide proper documentation on the services provided	2
Follow up with customer / user at a later date to verify satisfaction	2
Deal appropriately with customers' confidential materials	2

CompTIA A+ Practical Application Objectives Map

Topic	Chapter(s)
Domain 1.0 Hardware	
1.1 Given a scenario, install, configure, and maintain personal computer components	
Storage devices	11, 13
HDD	11
SATA	11
PATA	11
Solid state	11
FDD	13
Optical drives	13
CD / DVD / RW / Blu-ray	13
Removable	13
External	11, 13
Motherboards	3, 5, 7, 8, 9, 18, 20, 22
Jumper settings	9
CMOS battery	7, 9
Advanced BIOS settings	7
Bus speeds	8
Chipsets	7
Firmware updates	7
Socket types	3, 5, 9
Expansion slots	8, 9
Memory slots	6
Front panel connectors	9
I/O ports	9, 18
Sound, video, USB 1.1, USB 2.0, serial, IEEE 1394 / Firewire, parallel, NIC, modem, PS/2	3, 18, 19, 20, 22

Topic	Chapter(s)
Power supplies	10
Wattages and capacity	10
Connector types and quantity	10
Output voltage	10
Processors	3, 4, 5, 6, 8, 9
Socket types	3, 5, 9
Speed	5
Number of cores	5
Power consumption	5
Cache	5
Front side bus	5, 6, 8
32 bit vs. 64 bit	4, 5
Memory	6
Adapter cards	3, 8
Graphics cards	19
Sound cards	20
Storage controllers	3, 8, 9, 11, 12
RAID cards (RAID array – levels 0,1,5)	9, 11, 12
eSATA cards	3, 8, 11
I/O cards	3, 18
Firewire	3, 18
USB	3, 18
Parallel	3, 22
Serial	3, 18
Wired and wireless network cards	23, 24
Capture cards (TV, video)	20
Media reader	13
Cooling systems	
Heat sinks	5
Thermal compound	5
CPU fans	5
Case fans	5, 10

Topic	Chapter(s)
1.2 Given a scenario, detect problems, troubleshoot, and repair/replace personal computer components	
Storage devices	11, 13
HDD	11
SATA	11
PATA	11
Solid state	11
FDD	13
Optical drives	13
CD / DVD / RW / Blu-ray	13
Removable	13
External	13
Motherboards	3, 5, 7, 8, 9
Jumper settings	9
CMOS battery	7, 9
Advanced BIOS settings	7
Bus speeds	8
Chipsets	7
Firmware updates	7
Socket types	3, 5, 9
Expansion slots	8, 9
Memory slots	3, 6, 9
Front panel connectors	3, 9
I/O ports	3, 18, 19, 20, 22
Sound, video, USB 1.1, USB 2.0, serial, IEEE 1394 / Firewire, parallel, NIC, modem, PS/2	3, 18, 19, 20, 22
Power supplies	10
Wattages and capacity	10
Connector types and quantity	10
Output voltage	10
Processors	2, 5, 6, 8, 9
Socket types	3, 5, 9
Speed	5
Number of cores	5
Power consumption	5

Topic	Chapter(s)
Cache	5
Front side bus	5, 6, 8
32 bit vs. 64 bit	5
Memory	6, 9
Adapter cards	8, 11, 13, 18, 19, 20, 22, 23, 24
Graphics cards – memory	19
Sound cards	20
Storage controllers	8
RAID cards	11
eSATA cards	8, 11
I/O cards	
Firewire	18
USB	18
Parallel	22
Serial	18
Wired and wireless network cards	23, 24
Capture cards (TV, video)	20
Media reader	13
Cooling systems	5, 10
Heat sinks	5
Thermal compound	5
CPU fans	5
Case fans	5, 10
1.3 Given a scenario, install, configure, detect problems, troubleshoot, and repair/replace laptop components	
Components of the LCD including inverter, screen, and video card	19
Hard drive and memory	21
Disassemble processes for proper re-assembly	21
Document and label cable and screw locations	21
Organize parts	21
Refer to manufacturer documentation	21
Use appropriate hand tools	21
Recognize internal laptop expansion slot types	21
Upgrade wireless cards and video card	19, 21
Replace keyboard, processor, plastics, pointer devices, heat sinks, fans, system board, CMOS battery, speakers	21

Topic	Chapter(s)
1.4 Given a scenario, select and use the following tools	
Multimeter	10, 22
Power supply tester	10
Specialty hardware / tools	2, 10, 22
Cable testers	23
Loop back plugs	23
Anti-static pad and wrist strap	2, 3, 8
Extension magnet	2
1.5 Given a scenario, detect and resolve common printer issues	
Symptoms	22
Paper jams	22
Blank paper	22
Error codes	22
Out of memory error	22
Lines and smearing	22
Garbage printout	22
Ghosted image	22
No connectivity	22
Issue resolution	22
Replace fuser	22
Replace drum	22
Clear paper jam	22
Power cycle	22
Install maintenance kit (reset page count)	22
Set IP on printer	22
Clean printer	22
Domain 2.0 Operating Systems – Unless otherwise noted, operating systems referred to within include Microsoft Windows 2000, Windows XP Professional, XP Home, XP MediaCenter, Windows Vista Home, Home Premium, Business, and Ultimate, *Windows 7 Starter, Home Premium, Professional, and Ultimate.*	
2.1 Select the appropriate commands and options to troubleshoot and resolve problems	
MSCONFIG	17
DIR	15, 17
CHKDSK (/f /r)	12, 15, 17
EDIT	15

Topic	Chapter(s)
COPY (/a /v /y)	15, 17
XCOPY	15
FORMAT	15, 17
IPCONFIG (/all /release /renew)	23
PING (–t –l)	23
MD / CD / RD	15, 17
NET	23
TRACERT	23
NSLOOKUP	23
[command name] /?	15
SFC	15

2.2 Differentiate between Windows Operating System directory structures (Windows 2000, XP, and Vista, and *Windows 7*)

User file locations	4
System file locations	4
Fonts	4
Temporary files	4
Program files	4
Offline files and folders	4

2.3 Given a scenario, select and use system utilities / tools and evaluate the results

Disk management tools	
DEFRAG	12
NTBACKUP	17
Check Disk	12
Disk Manager	12
Active, primary, extended, and logical partitions	12
Mount points	12
Mounting a drive	12
FAT32, NTFS, *FAT64 (exFAT)*	12, *Win 7: 1*
Drive status	12
Foreign drive	12
Healthy	12
Formatting	12
Active unallocated	12

Topic	Chapter(s)
Failed	12
Dynamic	12
Offline	12
Online	12
System monitor	17
Administrative tools	4, 17, 26
Event Viewer	4, 17, 26, **Win 7: 7**
Computer Management	4
Services	4, 17
Performance Monitor	4, 17
Devices Manager	4, 8, 17, 19, 20
Enable	4
Disable	4
Warnings	8
Indicators	8
Task Manager	17
Process list	17
Resource usage	17
Process priority	17
Termination	17
System Information	4
System restore	4, 17
Remote Desktop Protocol (Remote Desktop / Remote Assistance)	4
Task Scheduler	4, 17
Regional settings and language settings	14
2.4 Evaluate and resolve common issues	
Operational Problems	17, 22
Windows specific printing problems	22
Print spool stalled	22
Incorrect / incompatible driver / form printing	22
Auto-restart errors	17
Bluescreen error	17
System lock-up	17
Devices drivers failure (input / output devices)	17

Topic	Chapter(s)
Application install, start, or load failure	17
Service fails to start	17
Error Messages and Conditions	4, 12, 14, 17, 26
Boot	11, 14, 17
Invalid boot disk	11
Inaccessible boot drive	14, 17
Missing NTLDR	12, 17
Startup	17
Device / service failed to start	17
Device / program in registry not found	17
Event viewer (errors in the event log)	17, 26, **Win 7: 7**
System Performance and Optimization	4, 17
Aero settings	4, **Win 7: 1**
Indexing settings	17
UAC	17, **Win 7: 4**
Side bar settings	4
Startup file maintenance	4, 17
Background processes	4, 17

Domain 3.0 Networking

3.1 Troubleshoot client-side connectivity issues using appropriate tools

Topic	Chapter(s)
TCP/IP settings	23, 25
Gateway	23
Subnet mask	23
DNS	23
DHCP (dynamic vs. static)	23, 25
NAT (private and public)	25
Characteristics of TCP/IP	23, 25
Loopback addresses	23
Automatic IP addressing	23, 25
Mail protocol settings	25
SMTP	25
IMAP	25
POP	25

Topic	Chapter(s)
FTP settings	25
Ports	25
IP addresses	25
Exceptions	25
Programs	25
Proxy settings	25
Ports	25
IP addresses	25
Exceptions	25
Programs	25
Tools (use and interpret results)	23, 25
Ping	23, 25
Tracert	23
Nslookup	23
Netstat	25
Net use	23
Net /?	23
Ipconfig	23
telnet	25
SSH	25
Secure connection protocols	22
SSH	22
HTTPS	22
Firewall settings	26
Open and closed ports	26
Program filters	26
3.2 Install and configure a small office home office (SOHO) network	
Connection types	23, 24, 25, 26
Dial-up	25
Broadband	25
DSL	25
Cable	25
Satellite	25
ISDN	25

Topic	Chapter(s)
Wireless	24
All 802.11	24
WEP	24
WPA	24
SSID	24
MAC filtering	24
DHCP settings	24
Routers / Access Points	23, 24
Disable DHCP	23
Use static IP	23
Change SSID from default	24
Disable SSID broadcast	24
MAC filtering	24
Change default username and password	24
Update firmware	24
Firewall	26
LAN (10/100/1000BaseT, Speeds)	23
Bluetooth (1.0 vs. 2.0)	24
Cellular	24
Basic VoIP (consumer applications)	25
Basics of hardware and software firewall configuration	25, 26
Port assignment / setting up rules (exceptions)	26
Port forwarding / port triggering	25
Physical installation	23
Wireless router placement	23
Cable length	23

Domain 4.0 Security

4.1 Given a scenario, prevent, troubleshoot, and remove viruses and malware

Use antivirus software	26
Identify malware symptoms	26
Quarantine infected systems	26
Research malware types, symptoms, and solutions (virus encyclopedias)	26
Remediate infected systems	26

Topic	Chapter(s)
Update antivirus software	26
Signature and engine updates	26
Automatic vs. manual	26
Schedule scans	26
Repair boot blocks	26
Scan and removal techniques	26
Safe mode	26
Boot environment	26
Educate end user	26
4.2 Implement security and troubleshoot common issues	
Operating systems	4, 14, 15, 16, 26
Local users and groups: Administrator, Power Users, Guest, Users	16, 26
Vista/*Windows 7* User Access Control (UAC)	4, 16, *Win 7: 4*
NTFS vs. Share permissions	26, *Win 7: 6*
Allow vs. deny	16
Difference between moving and copying folders and files	15
File attributes	15
Shared files and folders	16, 26, *Win 7: 6*
Administrative shares vs. local shares	16
Permission propagation	16, 26
Inheritance	16
System files and folders	14
Encryption (Bitlocker, EFS)	4, *Win 7: 7*
User authentication	16, 26
System	7, 26
BIOS security	7, 26
Drive lock	7
Passwords	7, 26
Intrusion detection	7
TPM	7

APPENDIX B

About the CD-ROM

Mike Meyers has put together a number of resources that will help you prepare for the CompTIA A+ exams and that you will find invaluable in your career as a PC tech. The CD-ROM included with this book comes complete with the following:

- A sample version of the Total Tester practice exam software with two full practice exams
- A searchable electronic copy of the book
- A complete list of the objectives for both of the CompTIA A+ exams
- A short video introduction to the Windows 7 CompTIA A+ exam objectives featuring Mike Meyers
- A copy of several freeware and shareware programs that Mike talks about in the book

The practice tests and video software are easy to install on any Windows XP/Vista/7 computer, and must be installed to access the Total Tester practice exams. The copy of the book and the CompTIA A+ objectives lists are PDF files, which can be read by Adobe Reader. If you don't have Adobe Reader, it is available for installation on the CD-ROM.

System Requirements

The software on the CD-ROM requires Windows XP or higher.

Installing and Running Total Tester

If your computer's optical drive is configured to Autorun, the CD-ROM will automatically start upon inserting the disk. If the Autorun feature does not launch the CD-ROM's splash screen, browse to the CD-ROM and double-click the Launch.exe icon.

From the splash screen, click the *Total Tester CompTIA A+ Practice Exams* button to install Total Tester. This will begin the installation process, create a program group named Total Seminars, and put an icon on your desktop. To run Total Tester, go to Start | All Programs | Total Seminars or just double-click the icon on your desktop.

To uninstall the Total Tester software, go to Start | Settings | Control Panel | Add/ Remove Programs in Windows XP or Start | Control Panel | Uninstall a program in Windows Vista/7. Select the A+ Total Tester program. Select Remove, and Windows will completely uninstall the software.

About Total Tester

The best way to prepare for the CompTIA A+ exams is to read the book and then test your knowledge and review. The CD-ROM includes a sample of Total Seminars' practice exam software to help you test your knowledge as you study. Total Tester provides you with a simulation of the actual exam. There are two exam suites: 220-701, 220-702. Each suite contains an exam that can be taken in either practice or final mode. Practice mode provides an assistance window with hints, and the ability to check your answer as you take the test. Both practice and final modes provide an overall grade and a grade broken down by certification objective. To launch a test, select Suites from the menu at the top and then select an exam.

Additional practice exams are available for both of the CompTIA A+ exams. Visit our Web site at www.totalsem.com or call 800-446-6004 for more information.

Accessing the PDF Copy of the Book and the CompTIA A+ Exam Objectives

You will find the PDF copy of the book and the CompTIA A+ exam objectives useful in your preparation for the exams. To access these PDF documents, you must have a PDF reader installed. If you don't have a PDF reader installed on your system, you can install Adobe Reader from the CD-ROM by clicking the *Download Adobe Reader* button. Once you have installed Adobe Reader, simply select *eBook* from the CD-ROM's splash screen then select the chapter you wish to read.

Technical Support

For questions regarding the Total Tester software, visit www.totalsem.com or e-mail support@totalsem.com. For customers outside the United States, e-mail international_ cs@mcgraw-hill.com. For questions regarding the content of the electronic book, visit www.mhprofessional.com/techsupport/.

INDEX

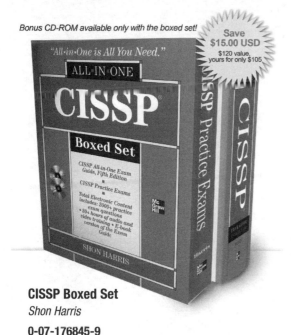

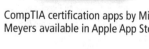
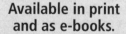